FAITH
TO RECEIVE GOD'S PROMISES

HOW TO "WALK" IN BIBLICAL FAITH
AND ALLOW THE BLESSINGS OF GOD
TO CHASE YOU

BY DR. RUTH TANYI

Faith to Receive God's Promises
Copyright © 2017 by Dr Ruth Tanyi.
Published by   Dr Ruth Tanyi Ministries, Inc
              P O BOX 1806
              Loma Linda, CA, 92354, USA.
              www.DrRuthtanyi.org

Cover design and Interior layout by: AJ Design

Additional copies of this book can be obtained from:
    Online: www.DrRuthtanyi.org
    Email: Info@DrRuthtanyi.org

All Scripture quotations, unless otherwise indicated, are taken from the *Holy Bible, New International Version®, NIV®*. Copyright ©1973, 1978, 1984, 2011 by Biblica, Inc.™ Used by permission of Zondervan. All rights reserved worldwide.

Scripture quotations marked NLT are taken from the Holy Bible, New Living Translation, copyright ©1996, 2004, 2007, 2013, 2015 by Tyndale House Foundation. Used by permission of Tyndale House Publishers, Inc., Carol Stream, Illinois 60188. All rights reserved.

Scriptures marked NKJV are taken from the NEW KING JAMES VERSION (NKJV): Scripture taken from the NEW KING JAMES VERSION®. Copyright© 1982 by Thomas Nelson, Inc. Used by permission. All rights reserved.

Scriptures marked AMP are taken from the AMPLIFIED BIBLE (AMP): Scripture taken from the AMPLIFIED® BIBLE, Copyright © 1954, 1958, 1962, 1964, 1965, 1987 by the Lockman Foundation Used by Permission.

We want to hear from you. Please send your comments and/or testimonies about this book to: Info@DrRuthTanyi.org or write to:

   Dr. Ruth Tanyi Ministries, Inc
   P O BOX 1806
   Loma Linda, CA, 92354, USA.

If you find any error in the citation of Scripture anywhere in this book, kindly contact us so we can make the necessary corrections, thank you.

ISBN 978-0-9986689-1-8
Library of Congress Control Number: 2017913372

All rights Reserved. No part of this book may be reproduced in any form without written permission from Dr. Ruth Tanyi Ministries Inc.
Printed in the Unites States of America.

CONTENTS

PART 1: Understanding Bible Faith

1   What is Bible Faith Anyway? 9

2   What are the Different Types of Faith Taught in the Bible? 23

3   What are the Different Characteristics of Bible Faith? 33

4   Why "Walk" by Faith? 45

PART 2: "Walking" in Bible Faith and Receiving God's Promises

5   How Do I Strengthen my Faith? 53

6   What are the Major Laws of Faith? (Part 1) 65

7   What are the Major Laws of Faith? (Part 2) 83

8   How Do I Know I Am Not "Walking" in Bible Faith? 101

Conclusion 109

Bibliography 113

Ministry Resources 114

About the Author... 118

INTRODUCTION

It is my opinion that the moment a person accepts Jesus Christ as their personal Lord and Savior, that individual, should immediately, within a few days or weeks, attend a basic Bible class on how to live out the remainder of the Christian Journey by faith. I believe that one of the main reasons why so many Christians become Carnal (i.e., make decisions based on their emotions, rather than what the Bible teaches) is because they have not trained their senses (ears, eyes, touch, smell, feelings) to be submissive to the teachings of the Bible, as a result of which they have weak faith. But for those Christians who want to experience the best that God has available for them, He has left us with only one choice: to live by faith in order to receive His countless blessings in this life — the choice is ours.

I believe that most Christians want to receive **All** of God's promises available to them in this life. But unfortunately, this is not the case, for various reasons. One of the major reasons is that many individuals do not quite understand what Bible faith looks like; and thus, do not know how to "walk" by faith as the Bible admonishes us to do. To this end, part 1 of this book will teach you what biblical faith is all about, and the different tenets of faith as taught in the Bible. In part 2, you will learn about the major laws governing faith as taught in the Bible, and the other practicalities of how to "walk" and live by faith daily.

Since God is a Spirit, we can only receive His promises as outlined in His Word by faith! I pray that upon completing this simple and straight forward teaching in this book, you will be edified, encouraged and strengthened to "step out" in faith and trust God with whatever you are believing Him for today, right now, in Jesus Name, AMEN.

Sincerely,

Dr Ruth Tanyi

DEDICATION

This book is dedicated to you, the reader! You are reading this book because you want to grow in your faith and relationship with God through Jesus Christ. Since that is the case, I trust that God has already rewarded your effort! And through His Holy Spirit, He will strengthen you step-by-step, thus enabling you to constantly operate in bold/active faith in order for His blessings to chase you, in Jesus name, AMEN!

Other Teaching Materials by Dr Tanyi to help you Grow with God through Christ

BOOKS BY DR TANYI:

- *Are You Moving Forward with Jesus? / How to Excel In Your Identity in Christ.*
- *Answers to the Toughest 25 Questions about the Real Jesus.*
- *Can I trust the Bible as God's Word? How do I Know? What Is the Evidence?*

COMING SOON!

- *13 Reasons Why People Get Sick! A Biblical Perspective & Remedies.*
- *Did God Really Say that? How to Overcome Doubt and Receive God's Promises: 10 Life-Changing Lessons Learned from Overcoming Metastasis Colon Cancer.*
- *A True Story of God's Unconditional Grace and Love: Healed by the Stripes of Jesus: My Story! My Miracle! How I Overcame Metastasis Colon Cancer.*

AUDIO CD TEACHING LIBRARY:

- *The Heart of True Christianity: The Gospel Message of Jesus Christ: Answers to 10 Major Questions Pertaining to Your Salvation in Christ Jesus.*
- *What Are the Gifts of the Spirit?*
- *Holy Spirit-Led Healthy Emotions: The Fruit of the Spirit and Your Health.*
- *How to Overcome Doubt and Receive God's Promises.*
- *13 Reasons Why People Get Sick: A Biblical Perspective & Remedies.*
- *Unforgiveness and Other Toxic Emotions: How to Walk in Forgiveness.*
- *Live Above Your Fears & Overcome Sicknesses and Diseases.*
- *Be Anxious No More.*
- *Daily Habits For Your Soul.*
- *Faith to Receive God's Promises / How to "Walk" in Biblical Faith and Allow the Blessings of God to Chase You.*

Grow in the Word of God and Receive His blessings through our Discipleship Bible Teaching Series.

The **Audio Podcast Series**, titled *"Biblical Principles for a Blessed Life,"* is an in-depth teaching through the entire Bible, from Genesis to the book of Revelation, focusing on major biblical principles, and teaching you how to apply those principles daily and receive God's blessings.

Biblical Preventive Health with Dr Ruth®
Biblical Preventive Health with Dr Ruth® is an educational magazine, which will educate individuals on how to integrate Bible-based principles into their lives, thereby preventing and overcoming sicknesses and diseases. You have heard what Medicine has to say! But do you know what the Bible says about a host of diseases plaguing people today? This magazine will teach you how to view your health from a godly perspective, and it offers practical recommendations to take care of God's temple.

13 Reasons Why True Christianity is Different: A Wall Mount Poster
This wall mount poster answers the question many individuals often ask: What makes Christianity different? This evangelistic poster will remind you daily of your unique relationship with God through Christ, and provide answers to confidently educate others and defend your faith. You will never be dumbfounded when asked to explain why your faith in Christ is unique, compared to other religions.

Obtaining Ministry Resources
To obtain additional copies of this book, or to get more information about the above ministry resources, please visit our Website:

www.DrRuthTanyi.org. You can also email, write or call us:

Dr. Ruth Tanyi Ministries, Inc
P O BOX 1806 I Loma Linda, CA, 92354, USA.
Email: Info@DrRuthtanyi.org
Phone: (909) 383-7978

PART 1

Understanding Bible Faith

CHAPTER 1

WHAT IS BIBLE FAITH ANYWAY?

The God of the Bible is a Spirit (1 John 4:8). Because no living human being has seen God, we must accept that He exists by faith. The Bible is very clear about this — it teaches that *"Without faith it is impossible to please God, because anyone who comes to him must believe that he exists and that he rewards those who earnestly seek him"* (Hebrews 11:6), (emphasis author's). Since faith is the primary channel by which we can receive anything from God, having a foundational and a solid understanding of what Bible faith is all about, is absolutely essential in our relationship with God, and how to receive His countless promises.

WHAT REALLY IS BIBLICAL FAITH?

In defining faith, the Bible teaches that: *"Now faith is confidence in what we hope for and assurance about what we do not see"* (Hebrews 11: 1), (emphasis author's). That definition was from the New International Version (NIV) translation of the Bible. Before I get into the details about this definition, let us take a look at how the Amplified Bible Translation renders this verse, which adds more clarity, in my opinion: *" Now faith is the assurance (title deed, confirmation) of things hoped for (divinely guaranteed), and the evidence of things not seen [the conviction of their reality—faith comprehends as fact what cannot be experienced by the physical senses]", (Hebrews 11:1),* (emphasis author's).

As you can see from the NIV definition above, the words "confidence," and "assurance" are a part of the definition of faith. This implies that, with Bible faith, there is some degree of "confidence" and "assurance" in "something" (to be discussed in the next section).

Then, I like the way the Amplified version added clarity to the definition of faith by using the words: " *title deed, confirmation,*" which according to the Webster Dictionary, means the "legal right to own something." Then, the "things hoped for" are "divinely guaranteed" (i.e., from God), and there is a strong conviction (i.e., certainty, persuasion) of the evidence of the "things not seen." As you can see above, the Amplified Bible concludes the definition by stressing how Bible *"faith comprehends as fact what cannot be experienced by the physical senses."* In other words, Bible faith completely accepts, as reality, the things in the spiritual realm, even though these things cannot yet be perceived or seen in the physical realm by our five senses! This is powerful!

Before I proceed, I want to clarify that the Greek word Pisteuo was transliterated (meaning to take a word from one language, and convert it into another word, in another language) from the Greek into the English language as to " believe." In the original Greek language, the word Pisteuo also means to have confidence, to be persuaded , to have a conviction and trust in something. In regards to the Bible, all of these are referring to belief or faith in Jesus Christ and/or the things of God. So depending on the Bible context, the word believe can be used to imply faith in God, Christ, His Word, etc.

Now, go back and take a look at the definition of faith from the different Bible versions listed above. Take note that the words: "Confidence", "assurance", "reality", and " hope" are all included in the definition of Bible faith. This brings me to an obvious question: Confidence, assurance, reality and hope in what? The answer is simple and straight forward: Confidence, assurance, hope, in the reality of a person: Jesus Christ. You see, confidence, assurance, hope, must all have an object of focus. And for the Christian, faith is a person: Jesus Christ, Who is the primary focus and object of our faith. In fact the Bible teaches that Jesus Christ is the primary author and finisher of our faith (Hebrews 12:2).

Since Jesus Christ is the author and finisher of our faith, it means that, the faith of a Christian is absolutely not a "blind faith" like some people have said. Our faith is steadfast on a real person: Jesus Christ, who was 100% God in the flesh and 100% human being like one of us; who lived on this earth over 2000 years ago; had a successful

> *Bible faith is based on 100% Truths: the known realties of the completed redemptive work of Jesus Christ on the cross. No wonder 2 Corinthians 1:20 teaches that All of the promises of God through Christ Jesus are a resounding "Yes" and Amen.*

ministry; died for the sins of the entire world, and was resurrected after three days as prophesied in the Bible. **Thus, Bible faith is based on 100% Truths: the known realties of the completed redemptive work of Jesus Christ on the cross. No wonder 2 Corinthians 1:20 teaches that All of the promises of God through Christ Jesus are a resounding "Yes" and Amen.** Because Jesus Christ was a perfect fulfillment of **All** of God's righteous standards, we can have 100% faith in Him and in His promises.

Let us examine the word "hope" in the definition of faith. The word "hope" as used to define faith is not a "positive thinking" or a "wishful thinking"; rather, it is hope in a person, Jesus Christ, and a hope that is 100% based on God's undeniable promises found in the Bible. According to the Webster Dictionary, hope is described as "feelings", "desires", "expectations", "wishful thinking", etc. All of these descriptions are linked to one's emotions. But for the true Christian "walking" in Bible faith, our feelings or emotions are not linked to our faith in God. For the Bible teaches us to walk by faith and not by sight (i.e., sight meaning living out our Christian life not based on our five senses, feelings or emotions), (2 Corinthians 5:7).

This is not to imply that something is wrong with our emotions: NO. The problem is that, our emotions are inconsistent and unreliable as a guide to lead our lives as Christians, because emotions fluctuate, depending on what is happening in the environment. Thus our emotions are not a true gauge of our relationship with God. Instead, we are to live and "walk" daily in accordance with the verifiable and proven Truths found in the

Bible, which is the authoritative, and Only inspired, infallible Word of God. These timeless Truths are consistent, just like Jesus Christ is; the author and finisher of our faith (Hebrews 12:2), who is consistent and stable, yesterday, today and forevermore (Hebrews 13:8).

SO FAITH IN JESUS CHRIST ABOUT WHAT?

You probably "got it", by now, that our faith is in Jesus Christ! But you may be wondering: Faith in Jesus Christ about what? Again, this is simple: Faith in **All** of His promises as outlined in the Bible, God's inspired and infallible Word to us. I really appreciate the way the Vines Dictionary of Old and New Testament Words summarizes the definition of faith: "... a strong conviction/persuasion of the things of God." I hope you are beginning to get a fuller understanding of what true Bible faith is by now?

For the Christian therefore, these "things of God" are the thousands of promises that God has made available to us in His Word because of His grace (grace meaning His unmerited favor towards us even though we do not deserve it). Although I have not personally done the calculation, I have heard several other ministers say that the Bible has about 6,000 (six thousand) promises from God to us. Even if the exact calculation is off, I am certain that there are at least over 4,000 promises specifically from God to us, which can be found in the Bible —this is amazingly awesome! Some of these promises include, but are not limited to: freedom from fear and worry; freedom from any kind of demonic oppressor/suppression; deliverance from all

Bible faith is when you believe in God's promises as specifically stated in His Word with all of your heart, then with confident expectation, you hope to perceive (i.e., physically see) the promise(s) with your senses, in God's perfect timing. Take note that the promises are already available to you; they are all done, finished, completed — you do not have to "earn" these promises.

sorts of addictions and carnality; the promises of eternal security; the presence of the Holy Spirit in our lives to lead and guide all of our decisions; the promise of our ability to hear the voice of God; and prosperity in every area of our lives, etc, etc, etc! The list is endless!

The great news is that, for the true Christian whose faith is solely on Jesus as his or her personal Lord and Savior, all of these promises have already been accomplished because of the precious and sinless blood of Christ. These promises are available to you in the spiritual realm, and by faith, you have direct access to them, to bring them into the physical realm, if you choose. Since God has given each one of us a free will (i.e., the ability to make our own decisions) to "walk" and live by faith, it is up to us to access these promises by faith, and experience their physical manifestations in our daily lives.

So simply put, Bible faith is when you believe in God's promises as specifically stated in His Word with all of your heart, then with confident expectation, you hope to perceive (i.e., physically see) the promise(s) with your senses, in God's

perfect timing. Take note that the promises are already available to you; they are all done, finished, completed — you do not have to "earn" these promises. Your role is to learn how to "walk" by faith and receive them, thereby bringing into manifestation the invisible promises of God as taught in the Bible into physical manifestation/reality, which can be perceived by your senses. But one thing is absolutely required to make your faith complete or perfect: your actions.

Your Actions will Make Your Faith Complete

The Bible teaches that faith without corresponding action is dead or useless (James 2:14-26). In context, the Apostle James is not talking about our Salvation in Christ Jesus, like some people have misunderstood this powerful teaching of faith out of the book of James. If you were to study James chapter 2 in context, it is obvious that the Apostle is teaching about putting into practice what we really believe as Christians, which is very consistent with the Apostle Paul's teaching in 2 Corinthians 5:7.

The action that makes our faith complete does not imply that we have to "perform" certain "deeds" before we would see the physical manifestation of the promises - NO. Our actions do not move God. God has already moved on the cross over 2000

The "actions" in regard to your faith is referring to you taking a step of faith (i.e., doing or performing some kind of action) which will be consistent with what you have already believed in your heart in the first place.

years ago in the person of Jesus Christ. If you depend on your actions to receive anything from God, you will not receive it, because that is considered "works righteousness" (see Romans chapters 2, 3 and 4), which is an affront to God. You must approach God only by faith in Jesus Christ, period!

The "actions" in regard to your faith is referring to you taking a step of faith (i.e., doing or performing some kind of action) which will be consistent with what you have already believed in your heart in the first place. Thus, you believe first in God's promises, then that initial step of believing will propel you to act according to what you believe. As an example, I am in my living room table right now writing this chapter. If I suddenly hear gun shots, and I believe in my heart (i.e., I have believed first) that it was real, I would immediately stop writing and run somewhere (i.e., acting on what I have believed) in my home to hide. That secondary action of running would be consistent with what I first believed in my heart (i.e., that someone was firing gun shots). So you can see how in this simple example, I would have only acted out (i.e, running away) because I first believed (i.e., that the gun shots were real).

On the other hand, using the same example, if I hear the same gunshots but I just continue to write without taking any action (i.e., running to hide), that would mean that I did not believe in my heart in the first place that the gun shots posed a real danger, hence I ignored it. Likewise, your action(s) as a Christian would be consistent with what you already believe, as stated in God's Word.

What is Bible Faith Anyway?

How Some Bible Individuals Perfected/Completed their Faith

Many biblical examples highlight this absolute truth that your actions are necessary to complete or perfect your faith in God. In Genesis chapter 22, the Bible teaches how Abraham obeyed God, and by faith, took his beloved son Isaac to sacrifice him on the altar. Keep in mind that Abraham actually took a step of faith to actually take his son to the location to kill him. While taking the boy to the mountain to be killed was a major step of faith and obedience, Abraham's faith was not made perfect or complete until he reached out his hand to take the knife to actually kill his son. That action of actually acting out his faith by pulling out the knife and raising his hand up to slay his son led to the physical manifestation of God's response and provision as seen in the Scripture below:

But the angel of the LORD CALLED OUT TO HIM FROM HEAVEN, "ABRAHAM! ABRAHAM!" "Here I am," he replied. "Do not lay a hand on the boy," he said. "Do not do anything to him. Now I know that you fear God, because you have not withheld from me your son, your only son." Abraham looked up and there in a thicket he saw a ram caught by its horns. He went over and took the ram and sacrificed it as a burnt offering instead of his son (vv. 11-13), (emphasis author's).

The example of Abraham teaches us how he had faith in God; believed that God will actually raise his son from the dead (Hebrews 11:19); and then he acted on what he believed (Genesis 22: 9-13). It was only after he acted on his faith that

God intervened. Had Abraham not pulled that knife in faith, the physical manifestation (i.e., God's provision of the sacrificial ram) would not have been evidenced.

The entire story of Moses and Pharaoh as recorded in Exodus chapters 8 through 11 also offers an excellent example of how our faith must accompany corresponding actions in order to be complete. If you were to go and study this entire "show down", you will notice that Moses had confidence, assurance and hope that God will perform mighty miracles as promised; yet, with each of the plagues, Moses had to complete/perfect his faith by performing some kind of action. Most of the time, Moses had to perform actions such as stretching out his arm to the sky, lifting the staff in his arm towards the sea, etc, which then led to the physical manifestation of the miracles, such as the parting of the Red Sea and the various plagues that destroyed the land of Egypt. Unlike Bible faith as just described , faith among unbelievers is different.

Two Major Categories of Faith

Based on the above descriptions of Bible faith, it is obvious that we have two major categories of faith: (1) Bible faith, a supernatural faith , which I have described; and (2) faith in the world, or faith among the unbelievers, which is considered "natural faith". Every human being has faith, faith in something, but the object of the faith is what differs. As an example, you had faith yesterday while you were driving on the freeway that you would get to your final destination safely, because you probably knew where you were going, right? You also have faith that when you get married, your spouse will love you back because you probably have dated him or her for some time, right? Or you have faith that when you take out a school loan to attend college for a particular area of study that has many job opportunities, you will graduate and have a job to pay back that loan, right, etc, etc. All of these are examples of a type of faith: Natural faith, faith in physical things that you have to first perceive with your senses before trusting and believing in the outcome.

> *Most unfortunately, the faith of an unbeliever is a true "blind faith", a "dead end", a "wishful thinking" and a "wishful hoping" for the best outcome, which often eludes them, leading to much frustration, fear, depression and anxiety. This is because circumstances often change, and everything in life apart from a relationship with the True living God of the Bible through His Only Son Jesus Christ is a "dead end", destined to crumble and fail, sooner or later.*

But as already explained, the object of the Christian faith is Jesus Christ, Him alone and nothing else. However, for many unbelievers, whose faith is purely natural or carnal, the object of their faith is often material things, such as their wealth, degrees, status in society, relationships with their spouses, children, etc. **Most unfortunately, the faith of an unbeliever is a true "blind faith", a "dead end", a "wishful thinking" and a "wishful hoping" for the best outcome, which often eludes them,**

leading to much frustration, fear, depression and anxiety. This is because circumstances often change, and everything in life apart from a relationship with the True living God of the Bible through His Only Son Jesus Christ is a "dead end", destined to crumble and fail, sooner or later.

As an example, an unbeliever who suddenly becomes bankrupt may experience unremitting depression, fear and anxiety for extended periods of time, and may not be able to rejoice, be thankful and maintain a godly perspective about the future (because they would be operating out of natural faith or carnality), until they are able to resolve the issue of bankruptcy and physically see their back account as positive, because their hope and faith was in their bank account.

On the other hand, a true Bible believing Christian who suddenly experiences bankruptcy, one whose faith and hope is in Jesus Christ and not his or her back account, would still be able to be joyful, thankful and rejoice in the Lord, because by faith, the individual knows that God's Word has promised that He is the source of all wealth (Deuteronomy 8:18). And the Christian would be aware that the same God that enabled him or her to obtain the wealth in the first place will do it again, because He is faithful. Do you see the major difference in perspective and attitude?

Again, the Christian operating in true Bible faith, which is supernatural faith, would rejoice and be thankful in spite of the calamities in His or her life; and while believing in God, he or she would step out in faith and start doing whatever is necessary to build up the wealth again, knowing all the while that God will open divine doors and bring the right resources and individuals in his or her path.

In conclusion, Bible faith is based on the verifiable Truths and promises stated in God's Word, which are available equally, to all true Christians because of God's grace. But each Christian must independently believe in these promises, then by faith access them, while carrying out corresponding actions as led by the Lord, and as stated in the Scripture, in order to perfect his or her faith, thereby bringing into physical manifestation God's invisible promises. In the Bible, we can find examples of different types of faith. I discuss these examples in the next chapter.

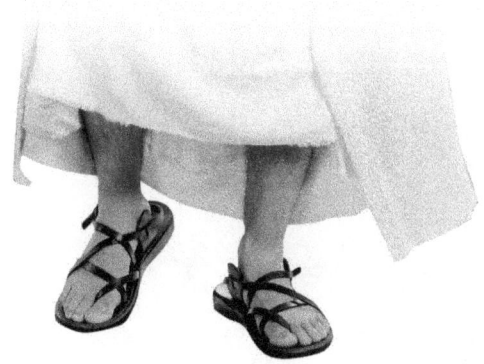

CHAPTER 2

What Are the Different Types of Faith Taught in the Bible?

It is necessary for me to clarify that the different examples of faith I am about to discuss does not imply that God has chosen, and thus decided that certain individuals should have "different" types of faith: NO. Rather, the Bible offers examples that we can glean from of how different individuals expressed their faith. Thus, based on these examples, we can discern different types of faith in the Bible.

Types of Faith Exemplified in the Bible

> **Saving Faith**

Romans chapter 10 teaches us that this type of faith is necessary for any individual to believe in Jesus Christ as their Lord and Savior. The Scripture teaches: "*If you declare with your mouth, "Jesus is Lord," and believe in your heart that God raised him from the dead, you will be saved. For it is with your heart that you believe and are justified, and it is with your mouth that you profess your faith and are saved*" (vv. 9-10), (emphasis author's). This is so interesting that we, human beings, were so destitute that we could not even believe God for

Salvation (i.e., being delivered from our Sinful Nature, and from the Kingdom of darkness belonging to Satan, and given a new life in Christ) for ourselves without His help. So God, in His love and grace, supernaturally made it possible so that when the Gospel message is proclaimed, those whose hearts are open and willing to receive His Truths can be emboldened, to step out in faith and accept God's free gift to Mankind: Jesus Christ.

For those of you unaware, the Gospel message is the absolute Truth that God Himself became a human being in the person of Jesus Christ, died on the cross, and was raised from the dead on the third day as prophesied in the Scripture. The death and resurrection of Jesus Christ overcame sin and death, and has paved the way, for each one of us, to, by faith, have a relationship with the Only True living God of the Bible, if we so desire. But this relationship is only possible when, by faith, you accept Jesus Christ as your personal Lord and Savior.

This teaching in Romans 10 verses 9 through 10 is very consistent with what I taught in chapter 1 about our actions necessary to completing our faith. Those individuals who independently ask (i.e., asking is the action) Jesus Christ to come into their lives after first believing in their hearts that He died for their Sinful Nature, will be completing their faith by their action of asking.

> **Temporary Faith**

In Jesus' teaching on the Parable of the Sower as recorded in Matthew 13, Luke 8, and Mark 4, an example of this type of faith is in operation. I will not teach and elaborate on this Parable in this book, I have done so in another book titled *"Are You Moving Forward with Jesus?"*, and in an audio CD teaching titled *"Overcoming Doubt"*. So those of you interested in an in-depth teaching of this parable should go to the resource list at the end of this book and learn how to obtain these resources.

But in brief, in the Parable of the Sower, Jesus uses an analogy of a farmer to illustrate a spiritual lesson. In this teaching, the Seed represents the Word of God; the Soil represents four different types of individual's hearts who will hear the Word of God taught or proclaimed; and the Evil one represents Satan, the Master thief. Jesus went on to teach that among the four types of hearts of individuals who will hear God's Word, the Word of God will have absolutely no effect on the first individual's heart, because Satan will immediately steal the Word from this person. Essentially, this type of person has zero interest in God's Word: it comes in one ear, off it goes out from the other ear.

The second type of individual hears the Word and is very excited, but this person has no roots. In essence, this is an example of someone exhibiting **"temporary faith"** in the things of God. This person receives the Word of God with much joy, but when trials and hardships come as a result of God and His Word, this person easily "gives up", thus he or she yields no fruit for God's Kingdom because his or her faith is shallow, weak and not firmed towards the things of God. This second type of individual described by the Lord teaches us a major lesson about faith — which is the fact that it requires time for our faith to grow and be strengthened.

The Lord Jesus went on to describe the third type of person in this parable. This third person is the individual who allows the "cares" of this world and the deceitfulness of riches to "choke" the Word of God, making it unfruitful. Again, this type of individual is not 100% focused on the things of God. His or her faith is only "**temporary**" because he or she allows "worldly or earthly things" to take precedence in his or her life, instead of God: Essentially, God is not first in his or her life. Then the last type of person the Lord described in this parable is the individual whose faith is consistent and stable in the Lord, as such he or she is able to yield much fruit for God's Kingdom.

I want to add that this **"temporary faith"** is not God's will for any of us, His children. His will is for us to grow in our faith, and be able to easily access His countless promises with boldness. Keep in mind that an individual exhibiting **"temporary faith"** is a person, who has, by choice, refused to allow his or her faith to grow and be strengthened.

➢ Intellectual or Dead Faith

The book of James (2:14-26) provides an excellent example of this type of faith. An example of a person exhibiting this type of faith could be an agnostic (i.e., a person who is unsure about the existence of God). Such individuals may even acknowledge that there is a "God", but it is just an intellectual knowing or acknowledgment, because they will take absolutely no action, such as accepting to receive Jesus' forgiveness and asking Him into their lives, in order to complete their faith. In such an example, the Bible teaches that it is useless, because even the devil himself believes, but he does not obey by acting and trusting God. This intellectual or dead faith can even be seen among believers, when they believe in the promises of God as outlined in the Bible, but yet refuse to act in faith accordingly, in order to complete or perfect their faith.

To illustrate, this could be a Christian who is believing God for physical healing, and he or she is actually believing and confessing with his or her mouth that Jesus has already healed him or her. Yet, he or she chooses to be bed-ridden, refusing to get out of bed when he or she is very capable of doing so. Such an individual would be exhibiting dead faith, because there is no corresponding action, such as getting out of bed and acting like an individual who is already healed. As another example, it could be a Christian who is believing God for a new job, but refuses to step out in faith and look for a job and/or take a less paying job—again, this will be dead or intellectual faith, which is useless without corresponding actions.

➢ Faithfulness

This is a noun, implying a state of being. Galatians chapter 5 verses 22 to 23 teaches that all true Christians have faithfulness in their new "born again" spirits. There are many Christians who erroneously go around saying that they have no faith: this is wrong. We all have faith, starting with "saving" faith, plus faith in our new nature (i.e., born again spirits). The problem is that some Christians do not use the faith they already have, thus their faith remains weak; I discuss more of this later in this book.

➢ The Gift of Faith

In 1 Corinthians chapter 12, the Bible teaches about the Gifts of the Spirit. One of these gifts is the gift of faith, whereby you become the vessel or conduit for God to work through, in order to manifest His miracles to others. Biblical examples of this can be seen in Joshua 10, whereby the Old Testament prophet Joshua commanded the sun to be still, and it did (vv. 12-13). This was also the case with Moses, who parted the Red Sea (see Exodus chapter14), and the Apostles Paul and Peter who raised the dead, etc.

I believe that the gift of faith is where many Christians get confused, thinking that since they cannot operate and perform all, or some of the miracles the biblical Saints performed, it means they do not have faith. This is incorrect, because the gift of faith is one of the gifts of the Holy Spirit, and not yours. Each

Christian has faith, like stated above, and we all have been given "the measure of faith" (to be discussed next), and with consistent godly efforts such as spending time in the presence of God, walking in obedience, holiness, meekness and willingness to be used by God, He can flow through you; and infuse you with His gift of faith, in order to perform His miracles. But it must begin with you preparing yourself as a vessel for God to work through, if you so desire.

As an example, when I was fighting cancer, I spent over 8 hours a day studying the Scriptures, praying, seeking God. And after about 11 or 12 months, I reached a point where I knew beyond a shadow of doubt that I was healed. And without anyone laying hands on me, my "little" saving faith and faithfulness in my born again spirit was strengthened, and I experienced God's gift of faith, which enabled me to receive my healing. It can happen to you too, regardless of what you are believing God for today!

➢ **The Measure of Faith**

Several Scriptures teach this principle. As an example, Romans chapter 12 states: " *For by the grace given me I say to every one of you: Do not think of yourself more highly than you ought, but rather think*

This implies that it is the same faith for everyone, the faith of Jesus Christ, although some individuals are manifesting or operating in more faith than others, because they are trusting God more and acting in faith.

of yourself with sober judgment, in accordance with the faith God has distributed to each of you" (v.3), (emphasis author's). It says "**the faith**", and not "a faith." There is a big difference between "a" which can vary, and "the" that is "constant". **This implies that it is the same faith for everyone, the faith of Jesus Christ, although some individuals are manifesting or operating in more faith than others, because they are trusting God more and acting in faith.**

Then in Galatians chapter 2, *the Apostle Paul wrote: " I have been crucified with Christ and I no longer live, but Christ lives in me. The life I now live in the body, I live by faith in the Son of God, who loved me and gave himself for me"* (v. 20), (emphasis author's). Take note that the Apostle is saying that he lives by "**the faith**" of the Son of God: Christ Jesus Himself. Then in 2 Peter chapter 1 the Apostle Peter wrote under the inspiration of the Holy Spirit: " *Simon Peter, a servant and apostle of Jesus Christ, to those who through the righteousness of our God and Savior Jesus Christ have received a faith as precious as ours: Grace and peace be yours in abundance through the knowledge of God and of Jesus our Lord" (v. 1), (*emphasis author's*).* What the Apostle Peter is saying here is profound, and can set a lot of you free, if you can meditate on this.

The Apostle Peter wrote this epistle to the First Century Christians, and it is still absolutely relevant to us, today. He was telling them, just like God is telling us today, that we have "**like precious faith**", as him, Peter, who performed amazing miracles, including raising Dorcas from the dead (Acts 9:32-43).

The Apostle Peter is saying that our faith is just like his faith, do you know why? Because it is "**the faith**" of Jesus Christ, the author and finisher of our faith.

I hope it is now obvious to you that all faith comes from God, but it is up to us how weak or strong we want our faith to be.

So the notion going around in the body of Christ that some Christians have more faith than others is very wrong and unscriptural. It is true that some Christians are expressing and "walking" by faith more than others, because they are fully committed to the Lord, and as such, they are experiencing more of His presence, power and miracles than others. This has nothing to do with God, but with us, and our ability or inability to access the promises of God: there is a big difference (I discuss how to strengthen your faith later in this book).

In conclusion, **I hope it is now obvious to you that all faith comes from God, but it is up to us how weak or strong we want our faith to be.** Before I discuss some "tips" on how to grow in faith and be strengthened, let us examine the different characteristics of faith as taught in the Bible. Proceed now to the next chapter for this discussion.

CHAPTER 3

WHAT ARE THE DIFFERENT CHARACTERISTICS OF BIBLE FAITH?

The ensuing discussion on the different characteristics of faith as exemplified in the Bible does not, by any means, imply that God has endowed certain individuals with a "specific" type of faith. Rather, the biblical examples below highlights how different individuals exhibit their faith in receiving from God. Although All faith, that is to say, the supernatural faith of the Christian, comes from God, some individuals in the Bible exhibited strong faith in their ability to receive God's promises, while others displayed weak faith.

Also, take note that in those instances where the terminologies of "little faith," "weak faith", " no faith", and/or "great faith" are used in the Bible, these are primarily referring to how individuals expressed their faith (e.g., see Mark 4:40; Matthew 8:10; Matthew 17:20). Therefore, as you proceed with the teaching in this chapter, remember that God is not responsible for our weak or strong faith, meaning, the way we express our faith. It is our responsibility to grow in our faith and be strengthened.

Weak/Passive Faith

This is an individual who is depending on others to help him or her to receive God's promises. When a person is brand new in the faith as a Christian, it can be understandable to depend on a mature believer in order to receive anything from God. But a time must come, that each one of us must go to God directly, in boldness, in the name of Jesus, to access His promises. We must grow in faith, because exhibiting a weak and/or passive faith is not God's will for any of us. We have some Biblical examples of this attribute of faith.

The Father of the Boy with Epileptic Seizures

In the Gospel of Mark chapter 9, we are told about the man who went to Jesus' disciples, asking them to heal his son from epileptic seizure, and they were unable to. But when he saw Jesus, he reached out to Him and asked for help. In telling Jesus his story, the father said, referring to the seizure: *"It has often thrown him into fire or water to kill him. But if you can do anything, take pity on us and help us"* (v.22), (emphasis author's). Here is the Lord's response: *"If you can'?" said Jesus. "Everything is possible for him who believes" (v. 23).* Then here is how the father of the boy with seizure responded: *Immediately the boy's father exclaimed, "I do believe; help me overcome my unbelief!"* (v. 24), (emphasis author's). As you can read from the Scriptures above, the father of the boy with the Seizure disorder was expressing a weak and passive faith. He had enough faith to call out to Jesus, but his faith was weak to receive the healing for his son without assistance; thus he acknowledged that he needed help, and the Lord went on to heal the boy.

The Man at the Pool of Bethesda

Another example of an individual expressing weak/passive faith is recorded in the Gospel accounts. The Gospel of John chapter 5 recorded how the man who had been invalid for 38 years was solely dependent on others (i.e., weak/passive faith) to help him into the pool in order for him to receive his healing. When Jesus asked him if he wanted to be healed, here was his response: *"Sir," the invalid replied, "I have no one to help me into the pool when the water is stirred. While I am trying to get in, someone else goes down ahead of me"* (v. 7). But here was the Lord's response to him: **"Get up! Pick up your mat and walk."** *At once the man was cured; he picked up his mat and walked* (vv. 8-9), (emphasis author's). As you can see from the dialogue between our Lord and the invalid gentleman, he was obviously expressing a very weak and passive faith, solely dependent on others. And of course, our compassionate and loving God, Jesus Christ Himself, went on and healed the man anyway, because he truly wanted to be healed.

STRONG/BOLD FAITH

An individual exhibiting bold/active faith (i.e., strong/bold faith which is manifested through actions, that is to say, active faith) is a person who has complete confidence in God's promises, while at the same time taking the necessary steps with boldness and a strong conviction (i.e., knowing in their heart) that God's promises will manifest in the physical realm. This type of faith will definitely yield godly results, because it pleases God. The Bible has several examples of individuals exhibiting this quality of faith.

The Faith of the Centurion

The Gospel of Matthew chapter 8 verses 5-13 records the incidence whereby the Centurion (a highly respected military personnel) came to Jesus to request healing for his servant who was dying at home. This Centurion displayed 100% confidence and trust in Jesus' ability to heal his servant. In response to Jesus inquiring whether or not He should visit his home to heal his servant, here is how the Centurion replied and displayed his bold faith: "...*Lord, I do not deserve to have you come under my roof.* ***But just say the word, and my servant will be healed.*** *For I myself am a man under authority, with soldiers under me. I tell this one, 'Go,' and he goes; and that one, 'Come,' and he comes. I say to my servant, 'Do this,' and he does it"(vv. 8-9),* (emphasis author's).

I have highlighted the Centurion's words above for you to see. This Centurion displayed amazingly strong, bold and active faith in Jesus, and completely trusted that the words of Jesus would be 100% sufficient to heal his servant. Jesus later commented about this Centurion's strong faith, and He healed his servant. This kind of display of faith will absolutely please God today, just like it did over 2000 years ago.

The Woman with the Issue of Blood

Another excellent example of bold and active faith is seen in the woman with the issue of blood (she was experiencing a bleeding disorder), as recorded in the synoptic Gospels of Matthew 9:20-22; Mark 5:25-34; and Luke 8:43-48. According to the Old Testament Law, this women was prohibited from coming to the public, because she was considered unclean due to the continuous bleeding she experienced. If she was found in public, she could have been stoned to death. But this woman had suffered with this bleeding disorder for quite some time, and had spent all of her money seeing the doctors but with no relief; she was still suffering. So when she heard of Jesus, she determined and purposed in her heart (i.e., had a strong conviction, confidence and assurance) that Jesus would heal her.

This woman was quite aware that if she was found out in public, she could be killed; she did not care, because she had 100% trust (i.e., believe or faith) in Jesus. So with that strong conviction, she acted on her faith, stepped out into the crowd, pushed her way into the crowd among hundreds of people crowding and following Jesus, and acted on what she believed and thought. For she thought and said to herself: "...*If I just touch his clothes, I will be healed." Immediately her bleeding stopped and she felt in her body that she was freed from her suffering*" (Mark 5: 28-29), (emphasis author's). This woman displayed an amazingly strong, bold and active faith, risking everything, even her life — this type of faith is still very pleasing to God today, and it will definitely lead to God's invisible promises to become visible in your life.

This type of bold and active faith is usually seen in individuals who get to the point in their lives where everything else has failed, and they finally come to the realization that if they do not turn to God 100%, they will not survive. Then as they focus on God 100% because everything else humanly possible has failed, and they have nowhere else to turn, they are able to receive from God. But it ought not to be this way. We do not have to waste time trying all other options, and then turning to God as the last resort; this is not God's will for us. God's will is for us to access His promises with such bold active faith right away, with whatever problems we are encountering today.

David and Goliath

Another excellent example of bold active faith is recorded in 1st Samuel chapter 17, where David, as just a young boy, was able to kill the giant Goliath who was over 9 feet tall, and had been threatening and scaring the Israelites (1 Samuel 17: 1-58). God was impressed with this type of faith, and is still impressed with it today!

Faith That Can Be Perceived

This is an interesting character of faith. In the Gospel accounts, Jesus was able to perceive that certain people had faith to receive their healing from Him. Examples of this can be found in Matthew 9:2 and Luke 5:17-20.

The Faith of the Paralytic Man and his Friends

According to Mark chapter 2, the four friends of the paralytic man had to, by faith, create an opening in the roof in order to lower the paralytic man's mat to the floor where Jesus was teaching, thereby bypassing the crowd. This was an amazing display of faith, and when the Lord saw (i.e., perceived) their faith, here is what He told the paralyzed man, *"Son, your sins are forgiven"*(v. 5), (emphasis author's). As you can see from the above example, Jesus was able to see or perceive the faith of the friends, through their actions, as they lowered the paralytic man to Him.

In my own ministry, when people come to me for prayer, I have been able to perceive when some of them are ready to receive from God. Those who are ready to receive are often calmed, focused, relaxed, their faith can be perceived in their body language and entire demeanor.

People can say one thing with their speech, but their body language would reveal their true intentions. Experts in communication say that body communication is about 85 to 90% of all communication. A person could say they are believing God for healing or another miracle such as finances, but if their body posture is slummed over, and they appear fearful, anxious, and are unable to relax; then in reality, an individual like this is not acting in bold and active faith — you get the point?

Faith that Can Be Heard

This is another "subtle" but powerful trait of faith as taught in the Bible. Second Corinthians 4:13 teaches: *"I believed; therefore I have spoken." Since we have that same spirit of faith, we also believe and therefore speak"* (emphasis author's). Those who are operating in true Bible faith are able to easily speak out their faith, because they believe in the promises in their hearts. In the Gospel accounts, Jesus teaches that out of the abundance of the heart the mouth speaks (Luke 6:45). Thus, peoples' words are a good indication of what is in their hearts, and what they are truly believing God for.

The Centurion and the Woman with a Blood Disorder

As already described above, these two individuals verbalized or "spoke out" their faith, after they believed in their hearts that Jesus was their healer. Granted, some people can learn to "talk the talk" but their actions, that is to say, their body language and their "subtle" body reactions will reveal their true beliefs. And those who are "faking" it by their words will not be able to sustain their faith over a prolonged period of time.

So biblically speaking, true Bible faith can be manifested in our speech, as we would be truly speaking what we believe. Jesus also teaches that whatever we first believe in our hearts, such as God's promises, if we speak them out of our mouths, it will come to pass. He said: *"Have faith in God," Jesus answered. "Truly I tell you, if anyone says to this mountain, 'Go, throw yourself into the sea,' and does not doubt in their heart but believes that what they say will happen, it will be done for them"* (Mark 11: 22-23), (emphasis author's).

FAITH THAT CAN BE TANGIBLE

By tangible, I mean some individuals' faith can be physically felt through a tangible object. In my opinion, this quality of faith is truly unfathomable.

The Faith of the Apostle Paul

Acts chapter 19 teaches that: *"God did extraordinary miracles through Paul, so that even handkerchiefs and aprons that had touched him were taken to the sick, and their illnesses were cured and the evil spirits left them" (vv. 11-12)*, (emphasis author's). The Apostle Paul "walked" in such strong, active and bold faith that even physical objects, such as aprons and handkerchiefs that touched him were supernaturally "encased" with his strong expression of faith —this is truly unfathomable; only God! But this kind of display of faith is still very possible to any of us Christians, today, because God is the same yesterday, today and forever (Hebrews 13:8), and we serve a God of impossibilities.

Faith with an Unwavering Confident Expectation

Another quality of Bible faith is that of an unwavering expectation in receiving God's promises.

The Faith of Moses

A classic example of this is the story of the Old Testament Saint, Moses. In spite of the challenges he encountered with Pharaoh as recorded in the book of Exodus, Moses displayed unwavering faith and confident expectation that God's miracles would be evident, and they were. Also, Moses displayed unwavering confident faith in God during those 40 years of wandering in the wilderness, and the hundreds of challenges he faced while dealing with the children of Israel.

This kind of confidence will engender hope, which will sustain the person as he or she stays focused on Jesus (Romans 5:3-5). This kind of hope yields godly results; and the power and ability to act in faith, just like Moses did during the destructive plagues that destroyed Egypt and Pharaoh (see the book of Exodus).

Faith Must Have Corresponding Action(s)

I have already discussed this character of faith earlier, but I will return to this quality of faith in Part 2 of this book. For now, I just want to add that, at times, the actions required to complete our faith can be as simple as obeying God's Word and forgiving someone, in order to experience that emotional deliverance and the peace of God that is eluding you. Or, it could be as simple as honoring and obeying God by supporting His work on the earth through your financial giving and/or services to advance His Kingdom on the earth.

In conclusion, God wants us, as His children to "walk" daily and operate in the highest level of faith: Strong/bold and active faith. You may wonder why? I present 5 major reasons in the next chapter.

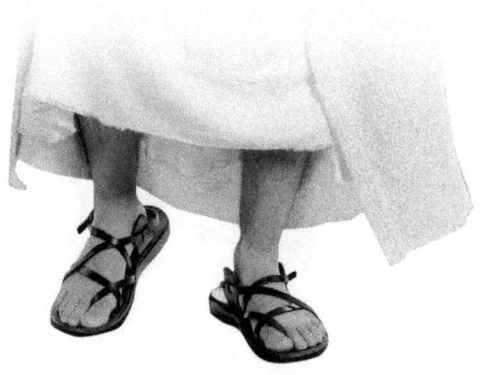

CHAPTER 4

Why "Walk" By Faith?

I am sure that by now you fully agree that without faith you will not receive anything, I mean, absolutely nothing from the Lord. While this is obvious, below are 5 major reasons why the Bible admonishes us to "walk" and live by faith daily.

True Christianity is a supernatural faith "walk"; a daily lifestyle habit, and so you would be wise to heed this advice from the Bible and learn to "walk" by faith daily. Even though I have mentioned some of these reasons in the previous chapters, I just want to highlight them here for clarity: Below are the 5 major reasons:

1. The Bible Teaches, from the Book of Genesis to the Book of Revelation, that Without Faith it is Impossible to Please God.

Hebrews 11 verse 6 specifically highlights this absolute Truth from God. So if you are a Christian attempting to receive anything from God based on your carnal abilities, you will not, and you will never succeed, because God will not recognize your efforts. You must surrender your ways of doing things and completely rely on God, in order to experience His blessings. Also, Hebrews 6 verse 12 emphasizes that we inherit God's promises in our lives through faith only. Then Hebrews 12:1 admonishes us to emulate the examples of the Patriarchs of Christianity, such as Abraham, Moses, Noah, who all "walked" by faith, experienced God's countless blessings in their lives, and died without even seeing the promised Messiah, Christ Jesus Himself.

2. *We Receive from God According to Our Faith.*

The Lord Jesus clearly taught us this in the Gospel (see Matthew 8:13; 9:22; 29). This is an interesting principle that many Christians fail to take into consideration when they are believing God for "something." This principle teaches us that it is never God who is the problem, but it is how we express our faith, that determines how we receive from Him. Essentially, we receive from God proportionately to how we believe, period!

As an example, if you are believing God for healing, and you believe in your heart that you will be healed when a particular Minister or Pastor lays his hands on you, then it is very likely that when that happens, you will receive your healing. Or, if your faith is in medications as your primary source to receive your healing, then God would likely work through the medications for the healing to manifest. Conversely, if you do not believe that it is God's will to heal you, then you will not be healed supernaturally by God, period!

This may raise an interesting question: what about those with weak faith, why do they still receive from God? The answer is that their hearts are "right"; they are completely believing God 100%, but they are just struggling with expressing strong faith. Remember that God deals with us based on what is in our hearts first. So in such cases, if the heart is solely dependent on God as The Healer (i.e., in cases when the individual is believing God for physical healing), God will see that, and He will, in His love, work through others who are operating in strong bold/active faith, or those operating in the gift of healings, for the promise or healing to manifest in the physical. This is what happened in the examples I described above with those expressing weak faith. But God's best is for us to express strong faith and receive from Him directly, rather than depending on others. But in His love and compassion, He has ways to reach everyone: the weak and the strong alike, while admonishing the weak to grow in faith.

I want to add that depending on others is okay. However, for those who are dealing with a terminal diagnosis, and medically speaking, have been given only a few weeks or months to live, depending on others can pose a challenge; if a fellow Christian operating in strong faith or the gift of healings cannot be reached in a timely manner. I know many godly Christians who have died prematurely because they were depending on some

Minister/Pastor to lay hands on them, and they could not reach the Minister/Pastor in a timely manner. Thus, God's best is that we grow in our faith, and learn how to operate in bold/active faith, in order to directly access His promises, in the name of Jesus.

3. God's Blessings Chase those Who "Walk" by Faith.

As much as God loves you as His beloved child, and is willing for you to be blessed and to prosper in every area of your life, Jesus made it very clear that only those who are operating in Bible faith will indeed receive God's blessings. After the death and resurrection of the Lord Jesus, one of His disciples, Thomas, refused to believe that Jesus had resurrected even after his fellow apostles told him they had seen the "Risen Christ".

Later, after about one week, Jesus appeared to Thomas. He said: *"...Because you have seen me, you have believed; blessed are those who have not seen and yet have believed"* (John 20:29), (emphasis author's). As you can see from our Lords' comment in this Scripture, He clearly taught that the blessings belong to those who believe by faith. This is a very powerful reason to "walk" by faith, if you want God's blessings to chase you. Today, we have many Christians frantically chasing after God's blessings, rather than allowing God's blessings to chase them. Jesus made it clear that if we "walk" by faith, we will receive God's blessings, period! So if you have not been experiencing God's blessings in your life, please evaluate if you have been "walking" by faith!

4. The Bible Admonishes Us to "Walk" by Faith.

Second Corinthians chapter 5 verse 7 is a very popular Scripture among Christians. It simply teaches: "For we live by faith, not by sight." This straight forward and simple to understand Scripture is powerful. In context, the Apostle Paul, under the inspiration of the Holy Spirit was teaching that in spite of the hardships round and about us, we should not allow our environmental circumstances, or what we perceive with our senses to mislead, direct or guide our decisions.

In essence, as Christians, we should have dominion or control over our circumstances and/or environment, and not allow external circumstances to rule us. Regardless of how dire our circumstances might appear, as Christians, we can stand in faith in accordance with God's promises and overcome, because God is for us. The Scripture teaches that God's promises in His Word are 100% true, and they will come to pass, in God's perfect timing, as we endure in faith.

5. The Bible Teaches that "The Just Shall Live by Faith."

This is a consistent theme across the entire Bible. Romans 1:17; Galatians 3:11, Hebrews 10:38, and many other Scriptures all teach this cardinal truth about the Christian journey as summarized in the book of Romans, from the New King James Version (NKJV) of the Bible: *For in it the righteousness of God is revealed from faith to faith; as it is written, "The just shall live by faith"* (1:17), (emphasis author's).

The "just" is referring to us, Christians, who have accepted Jesus Christ as our Lord and Savior, and have a relationship with God the Father. Because of our relationship with God through Christ, we have been "justified", meaning made as if we have never sinned. And God, in His love and grace, because of the precious blood of Jesus Christ, has forgiven all of our sins, past, present and future sins, plus absolved us from all of the consequences of our past sins. He will no longer judge us because of our sins, because our sins and its subsequent consequences and judgments were all placed on the sinless body of Jesus Christ on the cross. As such, we, the "just" must walk and live by faith, in order to please God.

Then under the inspiration of the Holy Spirit, the Apostle Paul also taught that: "... *just as you received Christ Jesus as Lord, continue to live your lives in him, rooted and built up in him, strengthened in the faith as you were taught, and overflowing with thankfulness*" (Colossians 2:6-7), (emphasis author's). This Scripture is teaching us that as we have received or accepted Christ as our Lord and Savior by faith, we should likewise live out our Christian journey by faith, rooted and grounded in Christ, who is the author and finisher of our faith.

Remember that the Christian life is a supernatural life, infused with power from the Holy Spirit as we obey and yield our lives to Him. Think about this for a moment: you never saw Jesus Christ physically before accepting Him into your life, right? You accepted Him by faith and believed in His promises. Likewise, that same child-like faith which you placed on Jesus at the time of your salvation, is that same child-like faith you would exercise or express daily, and allow it to grow and be strengthened, in whatever you are expecting to receive from Him today.

In conclusion, based on the above 5 major obvious reasons why we must "walk" by faith, God has not given us, His children, any other choice to know Him and experience His blessings. Thus, we must learn the practicalities of how to strengthen our faith daily, if we desire to please our Heavenly Father. I discuss some "tips" on how to do this on Part 2 of this book.

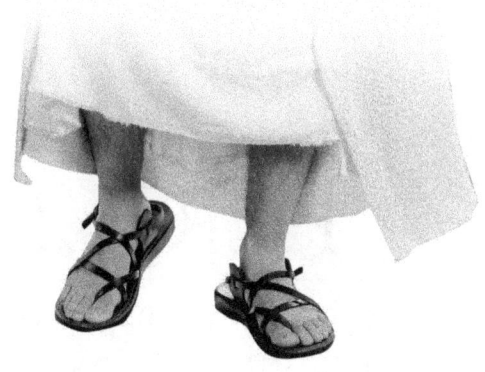

PART 2

"Walking" in Bible Faith and Receiving God's Promises

CHAPTER 5

How Do I Strengthen My Faith?

If you have been around the Christian circle for some time, you probably have heard so many Christians say that they do not have faith! Or you have probably heard others pray to God to give them more faith (i.e., increase their faith). Both of these positions are not biblical. Firstly, everybody has faith, like already described in Part 1 of this book; and secondly, praying for God to give you more faith is a wrong prayer of unbelief. Rather, you have to "use what you already have" and strengthen your faith, while allowing the Holy Spirit to guide your steps as you focus on Jesus, the author and finisher of your faith.

You Do Not Need More Faith

Jesus teaches us this principle in the Gospels. In Matthew 17, He taught: "... *Truly I tell you, if you have faith as small as a mustard seed, you can say to this mountain, 'Move from here to there,' and it will move. Nothing will be impossible for you"* (v. 20), (emphasis author's). I am so grateful that our Lord used a "Mustard Seed" as an example to teach us this principle of using our faith, because a mustard seed is one of the smallest seeds around, and in my view, it makes this principle very obvious. No, you do not need more faith, rather, start trusting God's promises by acting on them in faith, and completely believing God with the results, and your faith will become stronger.

Another powerful principle from this "Mustard Seed" example is that, it is not necessarily the "magnitude" of your faith; rather, it is the quality or "purity" of your faith that will enable the manifestation of the results you are believing God for. By "purity" or quality of your faith, I am referring to faith that is in operation in the absence of unbelief, doubt, fear, worry, carnality , and is 100% God dependent.

Every Christian is given "The Measure of Faith," remember? However, some Christians have trained their senses to trust God 100% in spite of the unbelief round and about them, and are pressing forward and believing God's promises whether or not they "feel" ungodly emotions of fear, worry, anxiety, etc. As such, these Christians are "walking" by faith beyond and above what they feel in their five senses, and thus have leant to "filter" unbelief

> *Take note that all of the recommendations to strengthen your faith as discussed in the ensuing section all lead to one final destination: <u>The Word of God</u>. The Bible teaches that faith comes by hearing the Word of God (Romans 10:17); this also includes studying God's Word. So these godly activities will keep your mind focused on God's Word, which will eventually strengthen your faith.*

out of their souls (i.e., their minds, thoughts, thinking processes, will, etc) and in their physical environment. Thus the quality of their small "Mustard Seed" of faith has been purified and strengthened. So, NO, you do not need more faith, just use what you have and "get rid of" unbelief, which is a "faith killer."

Take note that all of the recommendations to strengthen your faith as discussed in the ensuing section all lead to one final destination: <u>The Word of God</u>. The Bible teaches that faith comes by hearing the Word of God (Romans 10:17); this also includes studying God's Word. So these godly activities will keep your mind focused on God's Word, which will eventually strengthen your faith.

Overcome Your Unbelief

The primary way to overcome unbelief and doubt and strengthen your faith is to get rid of what I call "faith killers": Ungodly emotions, fear, anxiety, worry, impulsiveness, lack of self-control in your speech, fear of Man (i.e., people), etc. As long as you live in this "fallen world", you will always have countless opportunities to doubt the promises of God. But you have to decide, whether or not to believe God, or believe what your environment, friends, news media, your emotions, etc are telling you. The goal is not to strive for "perfection", that is to say, getting rid of all unbelief and doubt 100%, because it is humanly impossible to do so, since we live in a fallen world, and we have our "corruptible" bodies or flesh (i.e., we are finite), and we have an enemy, Satan.

Rather, the key is to learn how to believe and trust God in spite of the unbelief in your environment (i.e., walking by faith rather than by sight), and to learn how to overcome the unbelief and carnality round and about you, to the best of your ability, while trusting God. **Just in case you are wondering, unbelief in this context is referring to any other opinions, truths or ways of doing "something" that is contrary to what the Bible teaches.** Below are some recommendations on how you can overcome unbelief and strengthen your faith:

> *Reduce Environmental Toxins into Your Soul*

Your "soul" refers to your emotions, temperament, personality, and will (will meaning, your decision making ability). The Bible teaches clearly that bad company corrupts good manners (1 Corinthians 15:33). You would be very wise to heed this advice and reduce the amount of time, or even avoid individuals in your life who do not love or trust God, because their lack of trust in God will not strengthen your faith; in fact, their ungodly habits will discourage or weaken your faith. The book of Proverbs teaches that we should guard (i.e., protect) our souls, because out of it comes forth the issues of life (Proverbs 4:23).

You want to be certain to surround yourself with people who love God and encourage your faith, so that their godly examples can be rooted in your soul. Do not surround yourself with friends who will pour "toxic junk" into your soul in the form of fear, doubt and unbelief.

By avoiding or eliminating these environmental "toxins" into your soul, and spending more time in the Word of God, and with friends who love God and want to honor Him, you will be overcoming unbelief and doubt in your life, and strengthening your faith in God's promises and your ability to receive them in the physical realm. If you want more teaching in this area, check the resource list at the end of this book to learn how to obtain additional teaching from our ministry. We have separate audio CD teachings on how to overcome ungodly emotions.

➢ *Study the Testimonies of Others*

Another great way to overcome unbelief is to make it a habit to listen to, and study the testimonies of others; learning what God has done for them. The Bible teaches that we overcome by the blood of Jesus Christ and by the word of our testimony (Revelation 12:11). I call testimonies **"faith builders,"** because your faith will definitely be strengthened, as others' testimonies will encourage you to "step out" in faith and trust God likewise. If you do not know people in your immediate environment with true testimonies of God's blessings or miracles in their lives, go to the Bible and study the testimonies of the hundreds of Bible individuals that God used mightily, in spite of their flaws, such as the Apostles Paul and Peter, the Old Testament heroes such as Abraham, Moses, Gideon, Joseph, etc.

You cannot be 100% focused on God and your environmental fears and worry at the same time: Impossible, because godly emotions, such as peace, joy, trust, assurance, etc, and ungodly emotions and/or carnality such as anxiety, doubt, fears, etc, are mutually exclusive, they cannot co-exist at the same time.

As you diligently study the testimonies of others, it will build your faith to know that God can do the same for you as well — that is in fact the primary purpose of studying testimonies. God will use the testimonies of others to strengthen your faith; it works! When I was fighting cancer, I made it a habit to spend about 1 to 2 hours daily to watch DVD videos about testimonies of those whom God had healed from all sorts of various diseases, when medicine failed them. Boy, my faith was very strengthened, and I was able to overcome unbelief, as I constantly dwelled on God's goodness. Do likewise, and you will be strengthened as well, and your unbelief about God's promises will disappear supernaturally.

> ### *Engage in Constant Prayer*

Constant prayer, fasting, praise and worship are very powerful godly activities that will "crush" unbelief. The reason is that as you fast (i.e., deny yourself food or fluids for a set period of time while deliberately focusing on God) while in constant prayer, fellowshipping and worshiping God, your entire soul will be totally focused on Him and His thoughts, that alone will "squeeze out" unbelief and carnality from your soul effortlessly.

You cannot be 100% focused on God and your environmental fears and worry at the same time: Impossible, because godly emotions, such as peace, joy, trust, assurance, etc, and ungodly emotions and/or carnality such as anxiety, doubt, fears, etc, are mutually exclusive, they cannot co-exist at the same time. So as you deliberately stay focused on God 100%, you will be starving your fleshy thoughts and desires (i.e., carnality), and you will overcome unbelief and doubt, thereby strengthening your faith in God's promises, and positioning yourself to receive them.

> *Meditating on God's Word*

By meditating, I am not referring to just a casual reading of God's Word. Rather, a diligent and deliberate pondering and considering of what the Bible is teaching you as you read. This is another excellent way to get rid of unbelief. Romans chapter 12 teaches that we should not adhere to the ways of the world, or the ways unbelievers do things; rather, we should completely change our thinking patterns to be consistent with what the Bible says about us (v.2). You can only accomplish this through meditation, which is a quiet contemplation about the Truths in God's Word over a period of time, until those truths become a reality to you.

Once God's Truths become your reality, His Truths will "shifter" out doubt and unbelief, and easily position you to strengthen your faith in Him and His promises. And as you meditate on God's Word, practice imagining yourself already as the victor; see yourself as one who has already received whatever you are believing God for, because in the spiritual realm, you have already received it. But you must first conceive and receive it in your heart, before you can see it physically. Thus, as you engage in these godly activities in order to overcome unbelief, learn and practice how to use your small "Mustard Seed" of faith, obey and "step out" in faith and trust God with the results — you will be impressed with what God will do with what you have.

Use What You Already Have

As you take "small" steps in trusting God with whatever you are believing Him for, your faith will be strengthened, as you will begin to witness His faithfulness and provisions in your life. You are the determining factor to initiate that first step to trust God.

Using Your Small "Mustard Seed" of Faith

As an example, a person may set a goal to begin an exercise program of weight lifting three times a week over a period of 3 months. Let us say the person's 3-month goal is to lift 20 pounds on the upper extremity, and 30 pounds on the lower extremity. On the first week of this program, this individual will not be able to attain his or her goal of lifting 20 to 30 pounds, right? Rather, the person will slowly but surely begin with maybe 5 pounds, which most healthy adults can lift, thereby allowing the muscle to be stronger.

Then as the individual's muscle becomes conditioned and stronger with lifting 5 pounds, it will become extremely easy to do, as such, he or she must advance to the next level, probably 7.5 pounds. Then as the muscle is more conditioned, the person will be strong enough to lift 7.5 pounds, then 10 pounds, etc, etc. You get the picture, right?

Just like a person's muscle must physically be strengthened, thereby allowing them to advance to the next stage of weight lifting in order to attain his or her ultimate goal, you can do likewise in the spiritual realm. You would do so by taking "baby" steps in faith, while trusting God with His promises, and the Holy Spirit will reveal the next step to you, and you will be strengthened, step-by step.

A Step-By-Step Journey

Using healing as an example, let us assume that you want to start believing God for physical healing in your body — this will be a great goal, because it is God's will for you to enjoy good health (3 John 1:2). Plus, God has already provided physical and spiritual healing for you on the Cross when Jesus died for you. So healing is a promise available to you, but by faith you must access this Truth, so that it can become a physical reality in your physical body.

To begin therefore, you can start practicing how to receive this healing in your body. Thus, if you have a headache, instead of immediately running to your medicine cabinet at home and taking a "pill" right away to relieve your headache, how about trusting God for the healing of the headache first, rather than quickly taking a "pill"? To do that, the first step will be to find a healing Scripture from the Bible; there are dozens, such as Isaiah 53:4-5; Psalm 107:20; Psalm 103, etc, which clearly teaches that God is your healer. Next, you will pray the healing Scripture over your headache. Thereafter, as an example, pray something like this:

"Dear God, I thank you that you have already delivered me from this headache that is attacking my body right now. Your Word says that you are my healer, I am believing you, right now, that this headache will not reign over my body. In Jesus name, I ask this headache to leave my body right now. Thank you Father, that you have answered my prayer and this headache must exit my body. Thank you God, in Jesus name Amen."

Pray a prayer of faith like the one above and believe in your heart that God has already delivered you from the headache, and "rest" on the truth that God has heard you. Then move on with your day and trust God with the results. Based on the authority of God's Word, if you do not allow doubt and unbelief to overcome you, that headache will leave your body (see Mark 11:12-25). As you stand and believe God for this healing and experience the deliverance from that headache without medications, you will be strengthened, and emboldened to believe God for other serious illnesses in your body and other hardships in your life. You have to start somewhere, and physical healing is a good place to start because you can see the physical results.

Another good example is in the area of finances. The Bible teaches us that God is the one who enables us to gain wealth (Deuteronomy 8:18). So with this truth in your heart, you can step out in faith and start generating wealth, through your actions (i.e., acting out your faith), believing that whatever you lay your hands on will be anointed by God, because He is the One who will give you the ability to do so, and He will open divine doors for you. Therefore, If you are good at sales, get a sales job, and trust God with the results. If you have a desire to start a business, go for it, and trust that God has already blessed the business, as you act in faith and stay obedient while practicing godly principles in running the business.

In conclusion, as you do these godly activities while trusting God, your small "Mustard Seed" of faith will be strengthened, and the outcome will be joy and peace, because your mind will be steadfast onto Jesus, and you will be well positioned to receive abundantly from God. And remember, God can do exceedingly, abundantly according to the power that is in you — this power, is the power of faith (Ephesians 3:20). Now that you are ready to "step out" in faith and trust God, how do you operate within the confines of Bible faith? I discuss this in the next chapter.

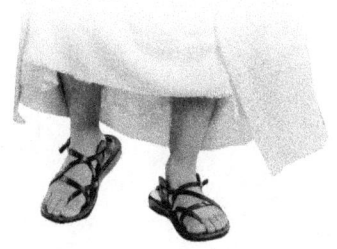

CHAPTER 6

WHAT ARE THE LAWS THAT GOVERN BIBLE FAITH? (PART 1)

I heard a story about a Christian man who was drowning and in his despair, he prayed and believed God for his deliverance. Shortly after he prayed, a Helicopter with rescuers came to rescue him, but he refused, believing that God will deliver him. Then another rescue team with boats came and made several attempts to rescue him, still he refused, insisting that God will spare his life. Then various swimmers sent ropes to pull him out from the water, yet he was still praying and trusting God.

Eventually, this man drowned and died. When he went to heaven, he asked God: "why didn't you rescue me? I prayed, had faith in you and believed because your Word says without faith it is impossible to please you?" In response, God said, "well, I sent all those rescuers to save your life, but you refused to accept my help. You refused to act on your faith. You wanted me to rescue you in your particular way, you did not truly have faith in me, that is why you are here before your time!"

Boy! I do not know how true this story is, but it highlights a major principle about "walking" and operating in faith: the Laws of Faith (see Romans chapter 3:27). The gentleman in that example operated outside the laws of faith, thus he "missed out" on God's perfect will for his life — he died before his time. This is not to imply that when we miss God's perfect will for our lives, we will die; No, that is not what I am saying. But, when we disobey God's laws and thus "miss" His perfect will for our lives, we will definitely encounter much pain and suffering, which, we will bring onto ourselves.

Most of you are probably aware of certain laws that govern electricity. One of those laws is the risk of being electrocuted if you were to step inside an open electric circuit while wet, right? Likewise, when you take a risk and attempt to operate in faith outside of the confines of the laws of faith, you will definitely be outside of God's will, which will prevent you from receiving from Him. And being outside of God's will means that your enemy, Satan, will have direct access to you, easily!

A person operating or "walking" within the confines of the laws of faith can only receive from God those promises that have already been made available to him or her by His grace.

OUR RESPONSE TO GOD'S GRACE

A point of caution is necessary before I discuss these laws of Faith. **A person operating or "walking" within the**

confines of the laws of faith can only receive from God those promises that have already been made available to him or her by His grace (grace meaning God's unmerited favor towards us even when we do not deserve it, because of our relationship with Jesus Christ). In other words, if God has not made available a promise to us in His Word, no amount of strong faith nor "walking" and living in accordance within the laws of faith will enable the promise to manifest! Did you get this? This is very crucial, because you cannot bring into manifestation something that God has not already promised to give to you as outlined in His Word.

To illustrate, I heard a story about a woman who lusted for another woman's husband. She took it one step further and actually acted out her faith by having an actual wedding ceremony by faith (without the man present), all the while believing that her strong faith would cause the man to divorce his wife and marry her. This was ridiculous! Although this lady displayed a very bold, strong and active faith, lusting and "stealing" another woman's husband is not a promise in God's Word, thus her strong faith could not manifest what she desired.

As another example, attaining money through fraudulent means and thievery in order to donate it to your local church or favorite ministry is not from God. In fact, this type of action will be

So keep in mind as we go over these laws, that Bible faith only brings into manifestation the promises which God has already (past tense) made available to you because of your faith in Christ.

from the devil. So no matter how much you want to support God's work on the earth, stealing and cheating "in faith" as a means to obtain money is an abomination to God, which He will not accept. **So keep in mind as we go over these laws, that Bible faith only brings into manifestation the promises which God has already (past tense) made available to you because of your faith in Christ.** Let us now examine these laws of faith.

Major Laws in Operating in Bible Faith

In my study of the Bible for this teaching, I came up with 16 major laws that govern how we should "walk" and live by faith, in order to appropriate God's blessings. These laws are like a roadmap as to how Bible faith should operate. There is no specific Scripture that lists all of these 16 laws I am about to discuss. Instead, I will refer you to different Scriptures that teach these laws.

Also, take note that these laws are not intended to be dogmatic; instead, they should serve as a guide to enable you to operate within the confines of Bible faith. Much more, keep in mind that there may be over 16 such laws, but I have grouped them into 16 major categories for simplicity. Below are the major 16 laws of faith, discussed in no particular order of importance, as each of them are equally important, and must be in operation concurrently for our faith to be made perfect or complete.

Faith Accepts Incomplete Knowledge of Facts

When operating in Bible faith, you do not need to have all of the data available to you before acting out your faith and trusting God. Many times, God may just give you a word, such as "go," or "stop", or "forgive", and you must act on it in obedience, before God will reveal the next step to you. You have to have a firm trust that in spite of the incomplete data you have, God will lead and guide you perfectly because He knows all things. **Waiting to get the full "picture" or a complete understanding about point A to point Z before acting in faith is absolutely useless, and is not considered Bible faith at all. Besides, God does not lead us by revealing the complete picture to us in advance.** As a general rule as seen throughout the Scripture, God leads and guides us step-by-step, as we obey Him.

Let us examine some biblical examples of this law. In Genesis chapter 12, God called Abram out of his family home and asked him to relocate to a foreign country, and by faith, Abram obeyed and started the journey, heading to a land he knew nothing about. All Abram had was an incomplete data to relocate. He had no idea what the foreign land looked like; just based on obedience to God, he acted by faith, and throughout his journey to the promised land, God revealed details to him step-by-step.

Another example is seen in Numbers chapter 21, when the Israelites were wandering in the wilderness. Due to their disobedience, God allowed venomous snakes to bite them and many died. Then, after much crying for help, God had compassion for them and He instructed Moses to place a bronze snake on a pole (this was an incomplete data to them), and He instructed them that anyone bitten by snakes should look at that pole by faith (i.e., the incomplete data or instruction), and by looking at the bronze snake, the person would be healed and lived. This was such an incomplete instruction or data; yet, those who were bitten, looked at the pole by faith and lived (vv. 4-9).

In the New Testament, Jesus Himself later taught us that the bronze snake on that pole represented Him (John 3: 14-15), "The Healer" and "The Redeemer", who later overcame Satan on the cross, delivered us from our Sinful Nature, and has been exalted.

The Israelites could not fathom how by just looking at a pole, they would be healed—but this is how God would at times instruct us. And by faith, we will have to obey and act in order to see the manifestation of whatever we are believing Him for.

Another excellent example of just trusting God with incomplete data or instruction is documented in Joshua chapter 6. The Lord told Joshua, *"See, I have delivered Jericho into your hands, along with its king and its fighting men. March around the city once with all the armed men. Do this for six days. Have seven priests carry trumpets of rams' horns in front of the ark. On the seventh day, march around the city seven times, with the priests blowing the trumpets. When you hear them sound a long blast on the trumpets, have the whole army give a loud shout; then the wall of the city will collapse and the army will go up, everyone straight in."*(vv. 2-5), (emphasis author's).

By just reading the instructions from the above Scripture, does it make sense to you, that marching around a city and sounding trumpets will lead to "anything"? Again, the ways of God are not the ways of man. So if God has given you any instruction today, as revealed in His Word and/or He has confirmed it in your heart, you would be wise to act on it by faith, before you will experience the manifestation of the promise and/or directions for the next step.

Faith Must Accompany Corresponding Action(s)

I briefly discussed this law of faith in chapter 1, but I want to add to the discussion here. Under the inspiration of the Holy Spirit, the Apostle James teaches that faith without corresponding action is dead (James 2:14-26), remember? I hope you recall! It is extremely relevant for you to know that the faith the Apostle James is referring to has absolutely nothing to do with your Salvation in Christ Jesus (I already explained this earlier, refer to chapter 1 of this book for details).

This law of faith is so crucial, that Jesus Christ, God Himself in the flesh had to provoke "faith in action" (i.e., He provoked people to act out their faith) in order to bring into physical manifestation the invisible promises of God the Father. In Matthew 12, Jesus asked the man with a withered hand to stretch out his hand (i.e., to perform an action to support or correspond with his faith of believing for healing), thereby enabling his faith to be complete. Jesus said to the man: *"Stretch out your hand." So he stretched it out and it was completely restored, just as sound as the other (v.13)*. In this example, it was in the act of the man stretching out his arm that the healing took place; a powerful example of faith in action, that is to say, acting out one's faith.

Another powerful example of Jesus provoking people to complete their faith through their actions before the physical manifestation is evidenced can be seen in Luke chapter 17: *Now on his way to Jerusalem, Jesus traveled along the border between Samaria and Galilee. As he was going into a village, ten men who had leprosy met him. They stood at a distance and called out in a loud voice, "Jesus, Master, have pity on us!" When he saw them, he said, "Go, show yourselves to the priests." And as they went, they were cleansed* (vv. 11-14), (emphasis author's).

As you can clearly see in the above example, the healing of the lepers occurred as they obeyed Jesus and were walking to show themselves to the priest. Take note that: "*...as they went they were healed*". So their physical healing only manifested when they acted on their faith by walking to the priest, again "faith in action".

I really hope you are getting this picture very clear in your soul, because they are many godly Christians who have a very passive attitude that "if God wills it, it will come to pass regardless". This is wrong and not a biblical teaching, because God's will for the believer does not always come to pass, because we have a significant role to play, which is obedience and acting in faith, in accordance with His Word and as we yield to the Holy Spirit's promptings and guidance in our lives. Besides, all you have to do is to study the Scriptures and the stories of the children of Israel, and it will become very obvious that God's perfect will for their lives did not come to pass due to their disobedience.

Thus, in whatever you are believing God for right now, by faith, trust Him, and act accordingly for your faith to be complete, and then trust God with the physical manifestation of the promises. Like I said earlier, if you are in bed sick right now, and you are believing God for healing, if you are able, get up and act like a person who is not sick, if you truly believe in your heart that you are healed! Talk is cheap. If you really believe you are healed, then do not act like a sick person!

FAITH WORKS THROUGH PEACE

Bible faith will engender the peace of God, which is a supernatural peace, because you will be focused on the source of peace: Jesus Christ Himself, who is the author and finisher of your faith. When you are operating in Bible faith, the Lord will keep you in His perfect peace as your mind will be steadfast upon Him, because you trust and believe in Him (Isaiah 26:3). All

> *As an example, an individual who is "walking" in Bible faith will not go around asking for a "million" opinions about whatever they are believing God for, you get that?*

true Christians already have peace with God because of our relationship with Jesus Christ, but to experience the peace of God is a whole different matter, because only those whose minds are completely focused and dependent on Jesus will experience the peace of God.

As an example, an individual who is "walking" in Bible faith will not go around asking for a "million" opinions about whatever they are believing God for, you get that? You know why? Because they will go to the Bible and look for the promise, and stand firm, while trusting God and allowing Him to lead the "right" people to their path.

FAITH WORKS AGAINST FEAR

This is an interesting law of faith. A person who is operating in Bible faith is very much aware that he or she is afraid, or that the fear emotion is "knocking at the door of his or her soul," but by choice, that fearful emotion is not allowed to rule or dominate the individual's actions. It is very essential for you to understand that true Bible faith acts against fear, or in spite of the presence of fear.

If you are waiting for all fearful emotions to subside before acting, you will never please God. You have to, by faith, step out and act even when you feel afraid. And as you start acting against the fearful emotion, while staying focused on God and trusting Him, the fearful emotion will disappear. So take steps of faith even in the presence of fear and just trust God with the outcome. As an example, give financially to support God's work whether you feel afraid of giving or not! Do not rush to quickly take that pain medication at the first emotion of pain whether or not you are afraid, pause and pray first! Call someone who has hurt you right now and forgive them, whether or not you feel the fear of rejection, resentment, etc; just do it while afraid and trust God. By acting against fearful emotions, you will be exhibiting and "walking" in true Bible faith.

This is an attitude of the heart; true Bible faith still acts, regardless of the presence of doubt and fear. You will acknowledge that your bank account is red, but by faith, you will thank God for His provision in your life and be joyful and be thankful before that bank account comes back into the positive. True Bible faith will still thank God for His goodness even when the divorce papers come and fear is present, or when the diagnosis says Cancer and the prognosis is Hospice. A person "walking" in Bible faith will acknowledge all the fearful emotions, but will be determined to keep his or her eyes on Jesus. Some of you may think that this kind of a heart attitude is not possible; but YES, it is, and this is what God expects from us, because we serve the Only True living God, The God of impossibilities.

Faith Works Through Hope

An individual "walking" in Bible faith and focused on Jesus will be very hopeful, because for the Christian, hope is a person: Jesus Christ. And this type of hope is enduring and supernatural, which will add "fuel" to your faith "walk."

Romans 5 teaches that: *we also glory in our sufferings, because we know that suffering produces perseverance; perseverance, character; and character, hope. And hope does not put us to shame, because God's love has been poured out into our hearts through the Holy Spirit, who has been given to us* (vv. 3-5), (emphasis author's).

As a Christian, your hope in Christ will build your character, ignite your faith to become stronger, and bolder, and will ultimately lead to action which will make your faith complete. You can never lose hoping in God! So how do you develop this type of hope? By spending time in the presence of God through studying His Word. So whatever you are trusting to receive from God today, keep hoping and standing firm while focusing on Jesus, it will come to pass! And remember, this is not a "wishful thinking" or a "positive thinking" like unbelievers do, but rather, our hope is based on Truth, the Truths and known realities of God's promises. Thus as you hope in faith, the promise will manifest in reality, eventually, if you do not give up.

Faith Works By You Asking in Faith

I mentioned earlier how passivity is not a quality of Bible faith. In fact, there is nothing passive about the Christian life; in essence, you cannot receive anything from the Lord by being passive. Even in our prayer life, we must ask, in faith, and trust God with the outcome. God who created us in His image, is aware that there are some of His children who will not want to ask for His help, thus the Lord Jesus teaches that we should ask, and seek God with our request, and He will answer (Matthew 7:7-8).

Like everything else with God, this asking, seeking and knocking must be in faith, because you trust in His promises. In spite of this admonition, there are many Christians who are very passive and do not even ask God for help, due in part because of wrong doctrine ; that is to say, they erroneously believe that God's will for their lives will automatically come to pass, thus there is no need to ask. I have already discussed how this type of thinking is grossly wrong and unbiblical, right from the "pit" of hell, from Satan, the master deceiver himself.

Even though God is Sovereign, omnipotent (all powerful), omnipresence (being present everywhere), and omniscience (all knowing), He has given us a free will, and He wants us to present our request to Him by faith —He desires to hear from us. So if you do not ask in faith, you simply will not receive, period! God will not violate your free will and allow His promises to automatically manifest in your life, you must ask in faith and in obedience, then take the necessary steps for your faith to be complete.

Not asking God and yet believing for the manifestation of His promise is gross spiritual laziness and passivity, which does not please God. It is, in fact a sure guarantee that you will not receive the promise you want. The Bible teaches us that we do not receive because we do not ask! (James 4:1-3). Also, many godly Christians are confused between "resting" in the Lord

> *But as Christians, "resting" in Christ is a display of strong faith, as we would be completely trusting in His wisdom, and avoiding disobedience and "works".*

and being passive. As Christians, it is very appropriate to "rest" in the Lord when we reach a point that we believe we have taken all of the necessary steps, by faith, as led by the Holy Spirit, in order to perfect our faith. When we honestly reach such a point, and there is nothing else in the physical to do, then we must "rest" (i.e., waiting on the Lord for the manifestation of the promise, in His timing).

The interesting thing is that "resting" and "waiting" on the Lord in this manner is a major display of faith, because as fallen human beings, we are naturally restless. **But as Christians, "resting" in Christ is a display of strong faith, as we would be completely trusting in His wisdom, and avoiding disobedience and "works"** (i.e., attempting to use your own human ability to "force" God's will to manifest) (Hebrews 4: 1-11). The irony is that, in many cases, it is only when we enter into God's "REST" that we, indeed, will see the physical manifestation of the promise. I have seen this happen several times in my own life, and I have heard many other testimonies to this effect.

Hopefully, you now understand that "resting" in the Lord should not be confused with passivity, whereby some Christians choose to do nothing, or refuse to act on their faith under the guise of "waiting" and "resting" in the Lord. Be bold therefore, and ask in faith. There are those who are even afraid to ask because of fear that God will not answer, or that the outcome would be negative; do not be afraid! God loves you, and He wants to hear from you: ask, seek, and knock, God is always willing.

And while "waiting" and "resting," continue to stand firm in prayer, ask for wisdom and direction and new revelation on how to proceed; and be patient. Who knows, it could be that your enemy, Satan, is hindering the manifestation of the promise! (Daniel 10:1-14). Or it could be that there is "something" in your environment, your life or circle of friends, such as unbelief, that is contributing to the delay of the promise manifesting. So be prayerful and seek wisdom regarding any hindrances to the physical manifestation of the promise: God will reveal it to you.

FAITH WORKS BY BELIEVING AT THE TIME YOU PRAY

Jesus taught that we should believe that we will receive the promise at the time we pray, and not later (Mark 11:24-25). This simple principle about the prayer of faith is often ignored by many. There are those who approach God in prayer with doubt and unbelief about what they are believing Him for. This attitude of prayer in and of itself is a primary reason for unanswered prayers. As God's children, a prayer of faith means that when we approach God in prayer, we have to first already believe in our hearts that the promise is available, and that He hears us, and

He will honor our request in His perfect way and timing (1 John 5:14-15). Then in humility and obedience, we have to approach God with confidence that we will see the physical manifestation of the promise, which is already available in the spiritual realm because of His grace. God will always honor prayers that are aligned with His Word, which is His will for us.

I recommend that if you cannot first believe that the promises are already available to you, and/or if you are experiencing doubt and unbelief about the promise, you should go to God first and ask for help with overcoming your unbelief and doubt. Thereafter, proceed to pray a prayer of faith, lest your prayers in doubt and unbelief will be useless — God will not answer such prayers, and you will not see the physical manifestation to the promise; you might as well not even bother to pray.

Faith Works by Confessing What You Already Believe in Your Heart

This is one of those laws that many people often ignore, yet we see this law in operation even in our Salvation in Christ Jesus. Romans chapter 10 teaches that if a person believes in his or her heart that Jesus Christ is Lord and Savior, then proceeds to confess it (i.e., speak or say what the person believes out of the mouth), the person will be saved (i.e., become a true Christian). This emphasizes the principle I taught in chapter 1, how the key ingredient to Bible faith is believing with the heart, then our actions and speech will only reflect what we already believe.

The Lord Jesus emphasized this principle by teaching that we only speak what is already in our hearts. Here is how the Lord said it according to the New Living Translation Version of the Bible: "*A good person produces good things from the treasury of a good heart, and an evil person produces evil things from the treasury of an evil heart. What you say flows from what is in your heart*" (Luke 6:45), (emphasis author's). When you are "walking" in Bible faith therefore, be certain to only allow out of your mouth those things or promises you are believing God for.

Watch your "tongue", and pray for God to enable you to put a guard over your mouth just like King David did (Psalm 141:3), because out of your mouth comes the power of life and death (Proverbs 18:21). Your words can either bless or hurt you, thus be certain to exercise self-control over what comes out of your mouth.

If you can learn to "tame" your tongue (James 3:1-12); that is to say, exert self control over your words, you will be well positioned to only speak God's promises over your circumstances, physical health, trials, etc, thereby fostering His promises to manifest in your life. Use your tongue to "curse" your enemy, Satan, and rebuke him. Do not use your mouth to speak contrary to what you want —God's promises. So think before you speak, and like the Apostle James teaches us, be quick to listen and slow to speak (James 1:19).

In conclusion, now that you are becoming more knowledgeable about these laws, are you beginning to discern some areas where you can grow in your faith? If you are like the average Christian today, the answer would be Yes. Because most of the times, as fallen human beings, there is always the temptation to "slip" into carnality and "walk "outside the confines of these laws; thus, make it your primary goal to meditate on these laws frequently, so that they will be rooted in your soul. Continue now to chapter 7 to learn more about the other laws that govern your faith.

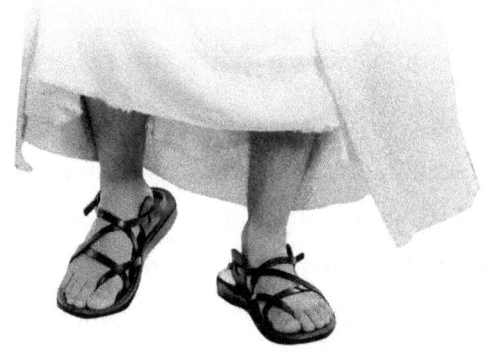

CHAPTER 7

What Are the Laws that Govern Bible Faith? (Part 2)

I am aware that there may be some individuals who may not appreciate all these laws that govern our faith "walk," because it requires obedience on their part. In my opinion, these laws are great, as God, in His love and grace, has provided to us, His children, through His Word, excellent examples that can enable us to easily receive His promises, if we so desire. Let us now proceed with the remainder of these laws, so that we can learn how to better "walk" by faith and appropriate God's countless promises available to us.

Faith Works By You Using Your Authority in Jesus Christ

Jesus said that apart from Him, we can accomplish nothing; essentially we are useless without Jesus (John 15:5). But the greatest news is that, as Christians, Jesus is always, I mean always with us , whether or not we feel His presence in our lives or circumstances (Matthew 28:20). Besides, we do not rely on our circumstances to dictate the presence of Jesus in our lives, anyway. And most importantly, even though Jesus has ascended into heaven and is seated at the right hand of God the Father (Acts 7:55-56; Romans 8:34; Ephesians 1:20), His Ministry as our intercessor continues, and He has given us authority, in His name, to accomplish good works on this earth (Matthew 28:18-20).

In Matthew 10, Jesus said: "*Heal the sick, raise the dead, cleanse those who have leprosy, drive out demons. Freely you have received; freely give*" (v. 8), (emphasis authors'). These are active verbs, requiring action on our part. Take a closer look at these active verbs again: "heal the sick", "raise the dead", "cleanse those with leprosy..." Think about this for a moment, Jesus did not ask us to beg God for healings, did He? No, He did not! Jesus did not teach us to ask the demons to leave us alone, did He? Absolutely No, He did not! Jesus did not teach us to beg God to heal us, did He? No, He simply said you should do it! He said "heal the sick," "cast out the demons", etc. You know why? Because He has given you, the Christian, the authority to use His name.

You have been given delegated authority to represent Jesus on this earth, and to enforce His will, just like a policeman has been given delegated authority to "handcuff" criminals on behalf of the judiciary system in most countries in the world today. Therefore, if you have true faith in the person Jesus Christ, and in His name, it will be Jesus working through you to heal the sick, raise the dead, etc, and not you —do you get that?

On your own, you cannot accomplish anything. But with complete faith in the redemptive work of Christ Jesus, and, in His name, while enforcing His authority, you can heal the sick, raise the dead, and accomplish many mighty works to glorify God. Unfortunately, many godly Christians do not know who they are in Christ, and as such, they have no clue as to the authority and power they have inherited in Christ. As such, they are unable to even lay hands on themselves, much less attempt to lay hands on someone else and believe God for healing. As a result of this ignorance, some of these Christians are running around searching for various Pastors and/or Ministers to lay hands on them, when they can do it themselves and get the same results. If you are struggling with who you are in Christ, I recommend you get my book titled: **"Are You Moving Forward with Jesus?"** I believe it will really help you, so check our ministry resource list at the end of this book for how to get that book.

A person operating in Bible faith is an individual who is acutely aware of who they are in Christ, and have confidence enforcing his or her authority, rebuking and overcoming the enemy, Satan, and commanding God's promises to manifest. There is a time for everything under the Sun (Ecclesiastes 3:1-8), which means there is a time to pray, a time to act in faith, and a time to say "enough is enough", if you discern that Satan is preventing the manifestation of the promise. If that is the case, you have to boldly resist Him (i.e., Satan) (James 4:7), and command God's promises to manifest in the physical realm in Jesus name.

> *It is not that Satan is stronger, No he is not, but God has given you authority, telling you that you should resist the devil, and he will flee from you.*

Think about it this way — if you are home and suddenly you see some strange person peeping into your window, then advancing towards your home to steal, I am certain that most of you would become very angry, turn on the alarm system and call the police immediately, right? You would not quietly allow a thief to steal from you, would you? Likewise, in the spiritual realm, when you sense that the thief, Satan himself, is preventing God's promises to manifest in your life, you must display a godly anger against him, and "kick him in the rear," by enforcing your authority and power in the name of Jesus.

It is not that Satan is stronger, No he is not, but God has given you authority, telling you that you should resist the devil, and he will flee from you. So you must fight, because Satan's primary goal is to kill, steal from and destroy you (John 10:10). You cannot allow him to do that!

I am aware that this may sound very strange to some of you, that you can enforce such authority to command God's blessings and/or miracles to manifest in the physical: Yes, indeed, and the Bible has many examples to this effect. Acts chapter 3 records an excellent example how the Apostle Peter did not even pray for God to heal the lame beggar at the Temple Gate. Instead, he simply enforced his authority and power in the name of Jesus, and commanded the healing to manifest, and the man was healed instantly (vv. 1-10). Here is what the Apostle Peter said to the beggar: *"...Silver or gold I do not have, but what I do have I give you. In the name of Jesus Christ of Nazareth, walk." Taking him by the right hand, he helped him up, and instantly the man's feet and ankles became strong. He jumped to his feet and began to walk. Then he went with them into the temple courts, walking and jumping, and praising God* (vv. 6-9), (emphasis author's).

Then in Acts 16, after several days of the Apostle Paul "putting" up with a demonic spirit that was manifesting through a slave girl, who was a fortune-teller, the Bible teaches that finally the Apostle Paul became so annoyed that he turned around and said to the spirit, *"In the name of Jesus Christ I command you to come out of her!" At that moment the spirit left her* (v. 18), (emphasis author's). You can see how the Apostle Paul finally got very irate and he finally enforced his authority in the name of Jesus.

Some of you may be thinking that those miracles happened because it was the Apostles Peter and Paul. If you are thinking like that, pause, and remember: We all have "like precious faith". All of us, Christians, have been given the same faith — The faith of Jesus Christ. So Yes, you can do likewise like the Apostles did, and use your authority in Jesus Christ!

Even when Satan is not responsible for delaying the manifestation, you can still enforce your authority in the name of Jesus and command the manifestation of God's promises in faith; this is scripturally an appropriate thing to do, because it will be Jesus Himself, working through you as the vessel. You have been given the highest privilege on earth, which is to call upon the name of Jesus; so use it, enforce it, and at times, as it is fitting, in faith, command the invisible promises of God to become a physical reality — this is your Kingdom right as a child of God. Do not allow anyone to deceive you otherwise, because there are several Christians, including some Ministers/Pastors who do not have a true revelation of their authority as a believer, and do not even believe that miracles are still happening today, which is FALSE! So, do not be deceived! Use your authority, and God will be pleased!

BIBLE FAITH IS SINGLE MINDED

A person operating in true Bible faith will not consider other alternatives — there will be no back-up plan. Such an individual will not have a plan B, except if God gives him or her the plan B. In my view, this law of faith is the most crucial, because you would have to completely renounce and/or denounce all other ways of attaining the manifestation of the promise, and trust God's way 100%. This is exactly what Proverbs 3 and many other Scriptures such as Romans 12: 2, etc, are teaching. Proverbs chapter 3 says: *"Trust in the Lord with all your heart and lean not on your own understanding; in all your ways submit to him, and he will make your paths straight"* (vv. 5-6), (emphasis author's). This is a very popular Scripture, and many Christians can easily quote these verses of Scripture, but putting it to practice is a whole different matter.

To completely trust God's ways 100% will be one of the most difficult things you will ever do in your Christian journey, but it will be the most powerful display of strong Bible faith, in my opinion. For you to do this, you would have to reach a place in your faith "walk" that you say like the Apostle Paul " let God's Word be true and every other person a liar" (Romans 3:4); and draw a line in the sand and be determined that it is either God's Word and His promises are true or they are not, and then you trust Him 100% and do not look back. Humanly speaking, this is difficult to do, but it is possible with the Holy Spirit on your side.

In fact, many people will experience the physical manifestation of God's promises when they reach this point in their faith, because there is nowhere else to turn. It is sad, that people have to suffer for extended periods of time before getting to this place of "no turning back" in their faith, when everything else have failed, and nothing had worked, and then they become desperate. We should reverse this process, and be determined to seek no other alternative but God, even before we become despondent and fatigued from trying out our own futile ways.

It is my belief that Americans are spoilt, and have too many choices to choose from; and as a result , many of them turn to God as a last resort, in desperation. But in some villages in the remote areas of Africa or elsewhere, where there is abject poverty, no access to healthcare and medications, when people get sick, they have no option but to turn to God. Hence there are testimonies of people in such remote areas experiencing major miracles and deliverance, just like those recorded in the book of Acts in the Bible, in the form of physical and mental healings, people being raised from the dead, etc. You know why? Because these people have no plan B. If God does not come through for them, they would be dead, period! Thus, they have trained themselves to become 100% God dependent, single-minded and focused on Jesus. Likewise, true Bible faith considers no alternatives and is single minded, rather than doubled minded. The Bible teaches that a double minded person (one who is wavering between two alternative positions, opinions, or ways of doing something) is not operating in Bible faith, and will not receive anything from God (James 1:8).

Faith Believes Nothing is Impossible for God

This is another very popular Christian phraseology: "nothing is impossible for God". We even have many Christian songs to this effect. But many Christians who say and sing this have a hard time actually believing this biblical truth. Those operating within the laws of Bible faith truthfully believe that "nothing is impossible" for God in their hearts, souls, and entire beings; it is not just a saying to them, but a true revelation because they have a firm conviction of this truth.

As an example, those Christians who do not believe that the types of miracles recorded in the book of Acts are still in operation today in the body of Christ (i.e., a collection of all Christians globally, regardless of denominational preference), would still tell you that nothing is impossible for God. Yet, they do not believe that people can be raised from the dead today! In my view, saying that "nothing is impossible for God," and then refusing that miracles, such as those in the book of Acts are still happening today, is a double minded position, which is not true Bible faith at all. You either believe that nothing is impossible for God or you do not, period!

What can help you to gain this firm conviction and faith that "nothing is impossible" for God is to gain a godly perspective about whatever you are believing Him for, such as the fact that all of God's promises to you are already accomplished in Christ and available to you. And gain the perspective that God has proven Himself throughout Scripture to be 100% faithful. He cannot lie; He is the same yesterday, today and forevermore. Thus if His promises have come true for others, it will come to pass in your life as well, because He is no respecter of persons, meaning he shows no favoritism (Acts 10:34; Romans 2:11). If you obey Him and practice His Word in faith, you will get His results, period!

Faith Displays an Unwavering Knowing that God is with You

This is another popular statement from many Christians: "I know God is with me." But here is the question: do you really believe that? Or is it all talk? If you really believe in your heart that God is really with you at all times, why do you quickly run to your friends and others for options and opinions instead of running to God first? If you truly believe God is with you at all times, why do you complain of loneliness all of the time, and you are attempting to use physical things, such as "ungodly relationships", "medications" etc, to "cover up" your loneliness, which are all futile attempts that will fail, anyway. These questions are not intended to offend you, but rather to help you to evaluate how truly you believe and are trusting God's promises in your life. Because many times, many people just say things without truly evaluating their deepest intentions. They say what they want others to hear and believe about them; but inwardly, they are afraid, lonely, depressed and defeated. Do not be angry with me for telling you this biblical truth. If you can humble yourself and receive this truth, it has the potential to "deliver" you from the fear of loneliness.

Individuals "walking" and living daily by true Bible faith have an unwavering supernatural knowing that God is with them, regardless of the outcome. Such individuals are very content, are not too focused on the outcome of the promise, but rather on their relationship with God, knowing that God is faithful. An individual operating in Bible faith knows beyond a shadow of doubt that God is his or her best friend, even when everyone else forsakes him or her. He or she firmly believes that God will never leave or forsake him or her (Hebrews 13:5; Deuteronomy 31:6). Such an individual believes in his or her heart that since God is for him or her, no weapon formed against him or her will ever prosper(Isaiah 54:17).

There are people who cannot even be alone for a day, much less two days because of fear. They always want to connect with a physical human being on a daily basis. They are unable to sit "still", or be quiet and listen to God. Some of the reasons include fear of loneliness, and fear that if they were to sit still and evaluate their innermost thoughts and life, they would have to question if there is more to life than what they are experiencing. I actually know people like these, some of my patients and others! If you are one of these people, then no matter what you say, you do not have a true revelation that God is always with you. Thus, I recommend that you grow in this area, because "alone" you came into this life, and "alone" you will die! Learn to have quiet times with God and trust His presence, this will be a good display of "walking" in the laws of Bible faith.

FAITH LOOKS FORWARD TO THE REWARD

Hebrews 11 teaches that after God called Abraham to relocate to a land He promised him, a land he had no idea where he was going to, by faith he was: *"... looking forward to the city with foundations, whose architect and builder is God"* (v. 10), (emphasis author's). Then we are told in verses 15 and 16 that if Abraham and his wife Sarah had longed for (i.e., had the desire to, or looked back to) the country they came from, they would have had the opportunity to return there (Hebrews 11: 15-16). What these verses are teaching us is that Bible faith looks forward to the promise, there is no "looking back". This is an amazing law of Bible faith! It will keep you hopeful.

Individuals who are believing God's promises do not consider the opportunities they "left behind". They make a decision to trust God, and that is it, no looking back, period!; regardless of the consequences! In order to gain this type of perspective, picture and imagine yourself as already possessing the promises just like Abraham did. Such forward and hopeful thinking is a powerful display of Bible faith, which is energizing. To practice this law, I recommend that you find a Scripture pertaining to the promise you are believing God for, meditate on it, and envision yourself as already successful, because you are in Christ.

As an example, in our ministry right now, I am believing God for financial resources to accomplish what He has placed in my heart for the ministry. Thus, I must operate in strong faith. And as a result, I have been meditating daily on Ephesians 2:10, standing on the promise that since I am God's co-worker on this earth, He has already prepared (i.e., pre-ordained) good works for me to accomplish. And since God is faithful, He will provide the financial resources through people, to bring to pass the things He has placed in my heart for the ministry. This is really helping me to stand in faith and endure, thus I am truly "resting" on this promise, and I am "looking forward" to the manifestation.

I recommend you do likewise: meditate on the promise you are believing God for, envision it as coming to pass and "rest." Because before you can receive anything from God in the physical, you must first conceive it in your heart and be ready to receive it. This statement may surprise some of you. But there are people who are believing God for promises, but they are unable to first receive it in their hearts. You can only receive a promise physically, if you first conceive and receive it in your heart. That promise which is already available to you in the spiritual realm has to become a reality first in your heart, then it will become a reality in the physical realm.

Faith Believes Above and Beyond Physical Circumstances

I have already explained this law in passing, so I will just make a statement here and move on. God cannot lie. His Words spoken in faith will bring forth results (Isaiah 55:11). An individual "walking" in this law focuses on the promises in God's Word, rather than the problem or circumstance he or she is experiencing. As fallen human beings, it is very easy for us to dwell on our problems, give them special attention, and easily ignore the Truth that God is bigger than our problems. When you are operating within the laws of faith, learn to refuse to ponder or meditate on your problems. Rather, meditate on the promises of God.

There is a general rule in life, which goes like this: whatever you magnify (i.e., give special attention to) in your life, it will become your reality. To illustrate, it is like using a magnifying glass to take a closer look at "certain sentences" in a book. What happens when you do that? The font size of the "certain sentences" will become larger (i.e., they will be magnified), thus enabling you to primarily see and focus on those sentences much better, while the other sentences in the book will "fade" in the background, right? This same principle is very true in the spiritual realm, with regards to the things of God. If you magnify (i.e., stay focused and give special attention to) God's promises, they will take precedence in your life and become your reality, and your problems will disappear effortlessly; you would do this by meditating on God's promises and the solutions to your problems. And as you do that, your problems will "shrink" in comparison to God's supernatural abilities. God is God, He is the absolute "boss"; He is in control, so relax and trust Him!

Faith Works Through Love

God is love. God does not give love: He is love in His very essence (1 John 4:8). The highest display of His love was seen on the cross, when God Himself in the person of Jesus Christ suffered humiliation, mockery and died for the sins of the entire world, and has paved the way for each one of us to choose a relationship with Him, if we desire. God's kind of love is unconditional love (i.e., Agape love). None of us human beings deserve this kind of love, but we are blessed in that we serve the True living God Whose very nature is LOVE. And the Bible teaches us that God's kind of love, that is to say, His perfect love, casts out all fear, worry, because there is torment in fear (1 John 4:18).

Bible faith works perfectly by you having a true revelation of God's love to you. If you have a heartfelt revelation of how much God loves you, your faith will " shoot straight up to the roof." Knowing and believing that God loves you to the extent that if you were the only person on this earth, He would have still died on that cross for you, will cause you to have much faith in all of His promises to you. And the biggest hurdles to most people's faith, such as fear, doubt, worry, has to disappear with a true revelation and acceptance of God's love to you; this is a powerful "faith builder" —The love of God to you!

In the first few years of fighting metastasis colon cancer, one of the things I did was to meditate on the love of God to me, to the extent that my faith in His promises was extremely strengthened. I figured that, if God loves me enough to die for my sins, then His promises of healing as expressed in His Word will come to pass in my life, if I did not give up. And indeed, as I meditated on His love for me, it became a revelation to me, which quickened my faith, and I was able to "rest" in His promises of healing. Today I am 100% cancer free after over 8 years. If you are struggling to comprehend how much God loves you, it could be why you may be struggling with believing in His promises. I recommend that you meditate on God's love to you until it becomes a reality, and your faith will be strengthened supernaturally.

FAITH IS ENDURING

Any individual who is "walking" in true Bible faith will not easily give up, because his or her focus will be on Jesus, who is the author and finisher of the person's faith. Many people easily give up because they begin to focus on their problems and circumstances. If you do that, you will definitely fail, but if you stay focused on Jesus, you cannot fail. The Gospels tell the story of how the Apostle Peter saw Jesus walking on water, and he asked Jesus to command him to walk on water towards Him as well, and Jesus said to him: "*...Come," he said. Then Peter got down out of the boat, walked on the water and came toward Jesus. But when he saw the wind, he was afraid and, beginning to sink, cried out, "Lord, save me!" Immediately Jesus reached out his hand and caught him. "You of little faith," he said, "why did you doubt?"*(Matthew 14:28-31), (emphasis author's*)*.

A major lesson to learn from this example of the Apostle Peter was that he had enough faith to believe Jesus' command and walked on water. But then, when he started to look at his environment or the circumstances surrounding the water, such as the strong winds, etc, he began to sink because he took his eyes off of Jesus. Likewise, when we take our eyes off of Jesus and start focusing, or even slightly looking at the circumstances round and about us, we will "sink" (i.e., be overcome by our problems). Focusing on Jesus also means that your hope will be enduring and supernatural, and the Bible teaches us that those whose hope is in the Lord will not grow weary (Isaiah 40:31). Therefore, I recommend that you keep trusting Jesus, and you will be supernaturally strengthened to endure as you wait patiently for God's promises to manifest in your life.

In conclusion, now that you are aware how to operate and "walk" within the laws of Bible faith, I am sure it would be easy to detect when you are outside the boundaries of these laws of faith, right? Just in case, let us examine some "clues" to warn you when you are outside these laws, that way, you would come back and walk in the "straight and narrow". The next chapter explains some of these.

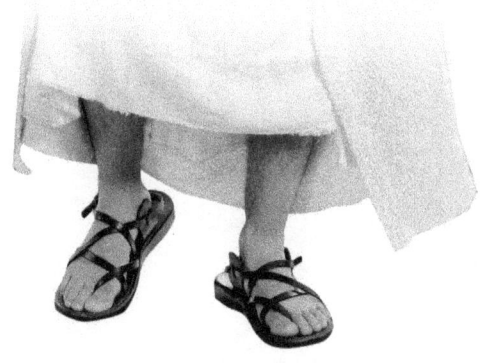

CHAPTER 8

How Do I know I Am Not "Walking" in Bible Faith?

As a general rule, as Christians, whenever we are not experiencing the peace of God, that should warn us that something is wrong. This "something" could mean several things for different people. But one major reason why some Christians may not be experiencing the peace of God is when they start "walking" outside the laws of faith. Thus, it is imperative that you gain some basic knowledge and understanding about certain "clues" that will serve as an alarm to you when you start delving outside God's laws of faith, that way, you would prevent yourself from much heartache, pain and suffering.

Some "Clues" that You are Outside the Laws of Faith

By now, I hope you are able to easily discern what some of these "clues" might be. Nonetheless, I want to still highlight them here for simplicity. To this end, below is a list of "clues", of

The only way to overcome these emotions is to focus on God, this is non-negotiable; nothing else will work. Anxiety medications will never cure anxiety; only Jesus is the solution.

ungodly/unrighteous emotions, behaviors, etc, to warn you. These are not meant to be dogmatic; but rather, to serve as a guide to help you to "turn on" your "spiritual alarm" when you start experiencing these deadly emotions. These include, but are not limited to:

✓ **Worry**

This is when you are chronically attempting to figure out things. In this state, you would not be trusting God but your own human ability, which is finite, and you will eventually fail. It is a dangerous place to be, because you will definitely limit God from intervening. You would be wise to **STOP, REPENT, and surrender to God**.

✓ **Anxiety, restlessness, panic attacks and the inability to control your emotions**

These emotions will definitely prevent you from "walking" in true Bible faith. Anxiety is never of God. It is either from your carnal thinking or from your enemy, Satan. The solution is simple: focus on God and be "still"; "rest" and wait on Him. Meditate on Scripture, be patient, and be patient! Your anxiety will not bring God's promises into manifestation any sooner; in fact, it will cause you to become sick. So you might as well just turn to the Lord.

The only way to overcome these emotions is to focus on God, this is non-negotiable; nothing else will work. Anxiety medications will never cure anxiety; only Jesus is the solution. If you need help in this area, our ministry has an audio CD teaching titled "**Be Anxious No More**"! This teaching has helped many others; it will help you as well. So go to the resource list at the end of this book and learn how to obtain a copy of this teaching.

- ✓ **Fear, and chronically thinking about a negative outcome**

This is another deadly emotion and a warning sign that you are "walking" outside of the laws of faith. Again, fear and negativity are never from God. You must learn to overcome fear, and the only antidote for this is the Word of God. Again the solution is simple: meditate on the Holy Scriptures.

- ✓ **Unforgiveness, bitterness, anger, resentment, jealousy, and being in constant strife**

You cannot operate in Bible faith when experiencing unforgiveness, bitterness, anger, etc. You must repent, overcome it and then "walk" by faith within God's laws in order to receive His promises.

- ✓ **Manipulating and using your own ability to bring God's will to pass**

Each time you find yourself attempting to come up with possible solutions that are inconsistent with God's Word, in order to attain His promises, you will absolutely be "walking" outside of the laws of faith. Stop it, be honest with yourself, and learn to trust and rely on God's ways. He knows best. If you "make it" to come to pass, you will be very sorry and miserable at the end.

Also, if you "force it" to happen, do not expect God to bless it, He will not! Which means you will have the burden to sustain it! Abraham and Sarah experienced unnecessary heartache , pain and suffering because they, with their own ability, gave birth to Ishmael (see Genesis chapter 15; 16), which was not God's perfect plan for them. Do not put yourself through such anguish! Allow God's will to come to pass, in His perfect timing — you will be very happy with the results. Remember, the blessings of God bring no heartache with it (Proverbs 10:22).

✓ Using your words to speak death over your situation and to others

The moment you start to use your words to speak negativity and "death "over your circumstances, then you will be delving outside the laws of faith. So repent, and watch what comes out of your mouth. The more you become conscious of what is coming out of your mouth, the easier it will become to exert self-control over your speech. For some people, this may mean repenting several times a day, but it is okay. As an example, if you are believing God for healing, only speak "faith filled" words such as the fact that you believe in your heart that Jesus has already healed you, whether or not you are experiencing symptoms of your disease! Because we "walk" by faith and not based on our senses, remember? So practice using your words to bring healing, restoration, and "life" over your circumstances.

✓ Wanting to give up too quickly

Experiencing the desire and or the need to "quit" too quickly is not of God, and it should serve as a sign that you are probably taking your eyes off of Jesus. If this is the case, become diligent in focusing on Jesus. Remember, our hope is supernatural and enduring, because it is a person: Jesus Christ. As you spend time with Him in His Word, your faith will become stronger, because faith comes by studying the Word of God and "staying" in God's presence.

✓ Your inability to overcome doubt and negative thinking patterns, such as the fact that God will not come through for you

Once you start to experience doubt, then know for sure that you are "walking" outside of the laws of faith. Quickly repent, and use the Word of God as the antidote to overcome doubt, so that you can start "walking" within God's laws of faith.

✓ The Fear of "Man"

When you start to consider what others are telling you more than what the Bible is telling you, you are in a dangerous position, and delving outside God's laws of faith. The fear of Man (i.e., people) will not honor God; in fact, it will "dampen" your relationship with God (Proverbs 29:25), who has your best interest at heart. So, when you start to contemplate and ponder people's opinions, that are contrary to God's Word, and they are causing you to "slow down" in your bold faith "walk" with the Lord, then you are definitely straying outside of the laws of faith. Stop, repent, and elevate God's opinions more than those of your fellow human beings, and God will in turn elevate you.

The list of "clues" can be endless, but the above examples should serve as an alarm that you are completely outside of the boundaries of biblical faith. These examples are not meant to bring condemnation, for there is no condemnation for those who are in Christ Jesus (Romans 8: 1). Thus, use the above examples as warning signs, or as an alarm to remind you that you need to repent, STOP the ungodly actions, and get back within the confines of these laws of faith, if you desire for God's promises to manifest in your life. _For those of you struggling with some of these ungodly_

Living by faith and "walking" within the confines of the laws of faith are governed by one major principle — your ability to discern and decipher God's Word correctly.

emotions, check our ministry resource list at the end of this book, because we have teachings that can help you to overcome these ungodly emotions.

LEARN TO DECIPHER THE WORD OF GOD

Living by faith and "walking" within the confines of the laws of faith are governed by one major principle — your ability to discern and decipher God's Word correctly. This is assuming that you have a relationship with God, because you have made Jesus Christ your personal Lord and Savior, and the Word of God is the final authority in making **All** of your daily decisions. If that is the case, then take a closer look at this powerful Scripture. Hebrews chapter 4 teaches that *"For the word of God is alive and active. Sharper than any double-edged sword, it penetrates even to dividing soul and spirit, joints and marrow; it judges the thoughts and attitudes of the heart"* (v. 12), (emphasis author's).

This Scripture is teaching us that the Word of God will enable us to tell the difference between godly and ungodly or unrighteous thinking patterns. Just by observing people's different statements and reactions to circumstances, you can use the Word of God to discern if their reaction is godly or not. The Word of God will also enable you to tell if your thinking patterns are consistent with the way God thinks of you.

For example, in a typical day, you will be bombarded with "millions" of thoughts, opinions, ideas, and various

> *Since there are "millions" of counterfeit ideas, truths, etc "out there", all you have to do is to study and know the real thing: The Word God. That way, when you are bombarded with a different opinion, you will be quick to immediately discern if it is of God.*

ways of doing a particular thing. But to accurately "walk" within the laws of faith, you would have to learn, through the Word of God, which ideas, ways, opinions are of God, yourself, the world, or from your enemy, Satan. And the best way to do this is by knowing God's Word through a diligent study of the Scriptures. **Since there are "millions" of counterfeit ideas, truths, etc "out there", all you have to do is to study and know the real thing: The Word God. That way, when you are bombarded with a different opinion, you will be quick to immediately discern if it is of God.**

Without you knowing the Word of God, it will be a challenge for you to apply the laws of faith I have discussed in this book into your life daily, and experience the manifestation of God's promises. So the best thing to do is to start studying God's Word daily, in order to become well equipped in discerning counterfeits that may be attempting to interfere with your faith "walk." With this thought, I now turn to the next page of this book with some concluding remarks.

Concluding Remarks

Bible faith is not a blind faith, it is based on known realties about the promises God has made available to us by grace, because of our relationship with Jesus Christ. As you are "walking" within the boundaries of the laws of faith, you will definitely experience godly results, in God's perfect timing. Be firm and steadfast, looking onto Jesus, because you are already an overcomer. First John chapter 5 tells us that: " *for everyone born of God overcomes the world. This is the victory that has overcome the world, even our faith"* (v. 4), (emphasis author's).

As a Christian, you can never lose: it is a win-win situation, no matter how you see it. If you die fighting and believing God for His promises, you still win because you will immediately go to be with the Lord. But if you live and overcome in this life because of your faith, you will still win, because it will become a great testimony for God : It is indeed a win-win situation, so take heart!

Remember the example of the Apostle Peter. He did not just "sink" at once into the water once he took his eyes off of Jesus; he began to sink, suggesting a slow process. Likewise, be warned! Ungodly emotions, doubt, fear, etc, should serve as an alarm for you to redirect your faith "walk" back within the confines of the laws of faith, lest these ungodly emotions will begin to slowly, but surely, cause you to start "sinking" into despair, defeat, and a giving-up attitude, which will not be God's will for you.

And remember to constantly strive to overcome "faith killers," so that your faith can be strengthened and emboldened, moment by moment, day by day, as you look unto Jesus, the author and finisher of your faith. And as you focus on Jesus, His blessings will chase you, effortlessly.

ACCEPT TO FOLLOW JESUS NOW

Throughout this book I have mentioned how God desires to personally know each one of us as His chosen children. He created us. He knows perfectly how we are "wired." He is the only one who truly understands. He loves us unconditionally, and His deepest desire is for us to know Him as well. He has made it possible for you to personally know Him. Because of His unconditional love, God became a human being, like one of us, through the supernatural conception and birth of Jesus Christ, who was God Himself in the flesh, in order to reveal

> *To know The True and Only living God of the Bible, you must come to Him through One way only — Jesus Christ, the Only person in the history of the world, who has met God's perfect standard of holiness 100%, and fulfilled All biblical prophecies perfectly.*

Concluding Remarks

Himself to us.

When Jesus Christ died on the cross, it was God Himself, expressing His unfathomable love to all of His creation, because He wants a relationship with you. **But, to know The True and Only living God of the Bible, you must come to Him through One way only — Jesus Christ, the Only person in the history of the world, who has met God's perfect standard of holiness 100%, and fulfilled All biblical prophecies perfectly.** Jesus Christ is the Only person who can give you what you are looking for: true joy, hope, peace, purpose in this life, and a secured eternity once you die.

Asking Jesus to come into your life is simply a heartfelt decision. So, if you believe in your heart that He died for your sins, and you are ready to confess this belief from your mouth, then the Bible teaches that He will accept you into His Kingdom, right now. If you are ready to accept God's forgiveness, and you need help doing so, say this simple prayer with me:

"Dear God, I thank you for sending your only Son, Jesus Christ, to die on the cross for my sins. I believe in my heart that Jesus Christ was God, who died on that cross for my sins, and was raised from the dead on the third day. I now receive your forgiveness of All of my sins, and I am asking you Jesus, to come into my life, right now, and change me. God, I ask you to fill me, right now, with your Holy Spirit, and teach me how to live as a Christian. By faith, I now declare that I am a true Christian, and I have denounced all other false gods in my life. Thank you God, in Jesus name, AMEN".

If you said the above prayer genuinely, from your heart,

based on the authority of the Bible, which is the Only inspired, infallible and inerrant Word of God, I declare you a true Christian, today.

Welcome to the Kingdom of light, God's Kingdom. If you would like, please contact us so we can send you more material to help you grow in your journey with God through Christ, and the enabling of the Holy Spirit, in Jesus name, AMEN!

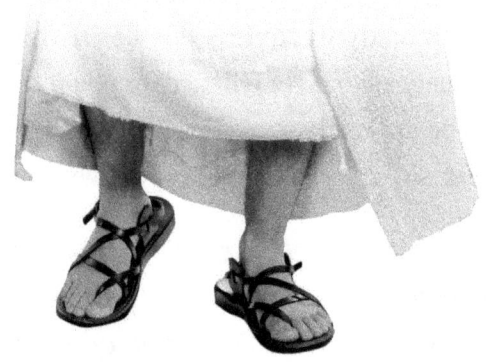

BIBLIOGRAPHY

W. E. Vine, Merrill F. Unger, William White, Jr. Vine's Complete Expository Dictionary of Old and New Testament Words. Nashville: Nelson, 1996.

Webster Dictionary: https://www.merriam-webster.com

OTHER BOOKS BY DR TANYI

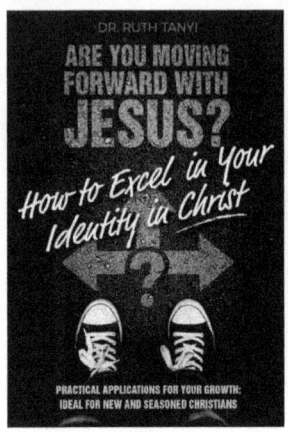  

Are You Moving Forward with Jesus? How to Excel In Your Identity in Christ

Answers to the Toughest 25 Questions about the "Real Jesus"

Can I Trust the Bible as God's Word? How do I Know? What Is the Evidence?

COMING SOON!

13 Reasons why People Get Sick! A Biblical Perspective & Remedies

Did God Really Say that? How to Overcome Doubt and Receive God's Promises: 10 Life-Changing Lessons Learned from Overcoming Metastasis Colon Cancer.

Healed by the Stripes of Jesus: A True Story of God's Unconditional Grace and Love: My Story! My Miracle! How I Overcame Metastasis Colon Cancer: You can Be Healed Too!

AUDIO CD TEACHING LIBRARY

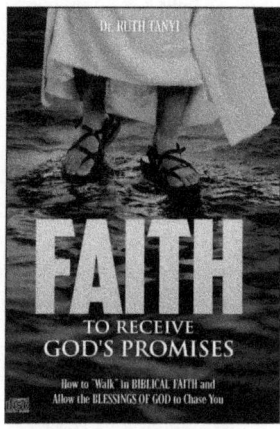
Faith to Receive God's Promises: How to "Walk" in Biblical Faith and Allow the Blessings of God to Chase You

The Heart of True Christianity: The Gospel Message of Jesus Christ: Answers to 10 Major Questions Pertaining to Your Salvation in Christ Jesus

What Are the Gifts of the Spirit?

Holy Spirit-Led Healthy Emotions: The Fruit of the Spirit and Your Health

How to Overcome Doubt and Receive God's Promises

13 Reasons Why People Get Sick: A Biblical Perspective & Remedies

AUDIO CD TEACHING LIBRARY

Unforgiveness and Other Toxic Emotions: How to Walk in Forgiveness

Live Above Your Fears & Overcome Sicknesses and Diseases

Be Anxious No More

Daily Habits For Your Soul

OTHER TEACHINGS BY DR TANYI

Discipleship Bible Teaching Series

Biblical Preventive Health with Dr Ruth ® Magazine

13 Reasons Why True Christianity is Different: A Wall Mount Poster
A Call to Action Poster

Visit **Dr Ruth Tanyi Ministries YouTube Channel** and watch our FREE Devotional Teachings, Plus Other FREE Teachings at your convenience, 24/7. Subscribe to our YouTube Channel and start enjoying our Free Teachings Today.

Visit www.Drruthtanyi.org/blog and watch our FREE Devotional Teachings.

Obtaining Ministry Resources

To get more information about the above ministry resources, please visit our Website: **www.DrRuthTanyi.org**

Contact Information
You Can also Email or Contact us:

Dr Ruth Tanyi Ministries, Inc
P O BOX 1806
Loma Linda, CA, 92354, USA
Email: Info@DrRuthtanyi.org

About The Author

Dr. Ruth Tanyi, DrPH, NP, ACSM HFS; CNS; MA Ministry

Dr. Ruth Tanyi is a Bible Teacher, Doctor of Preventive Care/Integrative Medicine, Board Certified Nutritionist and Exercise Physiologist. She is the founder /CEO of Dr. Ruth Tanyi Ministries, a non-denominational Christian, non-profit ministry located in San Bernardino, California, with primary focus on spreading the uncompromising Gospel of Jesus Christ; sharing God's unconditional love and grace, while concurrently teaching others how to integrate Bible-based principles with medical lifestyle practices in order to prevent and overcome diseases.

Even before being healed by God from metastasis colon cancer and other diseases in 2009, Dr Ruth felt called by God into ministry. However, since her healing and experiential knowledge and revelation of the love and grace of God, she has become an ardent student and teacher of the Word of God.

Dr Ruth's greatest desire is to tell others about God's unconditional love and grace, which she supernaturally experienced, and to teach individuals the lessons she learnt from God on how she received her healing, thereby helping others to be set free as well. Since God is no respecter of persons, Dr Ruth wants to strengthen others by reminding them that if God can heal her, He (God), can set them free as well regardless of the doctor's diagnosis or prognosis: All things are possible with God.

Dr Ruth is a public speaker and author, and offers a CD and DVD teaching library in addition to books on various topics ranging from the essential doctrines of true Christianity, to teachings on the very essential connection between God's Word and Medicine. Dr Ruth is also actively involved in the Body of Christ via her involvement with other ministries in advancing the Gospel of Jesus Christ, and in espousing the necessity of knowing God's Word. She considers herself to be a non-denominational Bible believing Christian, with a deep desire to fellowship and work with fellow brothers and sisters in Christ, regardless of denominational differences, for the common goal of advancing God's Kingdom and proclaiming the Gospel Message of Jesus Christ in these last days.

Prior to her calling into ministry, she had produced numerous TV series on lifestyle practices and disease prevention which aired throughout Southern California, and are still broadcasting through various media such as True Health Broadcasting Network, and SmartLifestyleTV, a division of LLBN Network worldwide. Her award winning TV series "Bad Sugar"® which focused on Diabetes, in addition to her other TV teachings on lifestyle and disease prevention continues to change thousands of lives.

Dr Tanyi has published numerous academic peer-reviewed journal articles and research papers, and she continues to serve as external reviewer for various International academic peer-reviewed journals. She is still pursuing her academic research in the area of lifestyle practices in preventing and overcoming depression. She has been nominated and selected in WHO IS WHO IN AMERICA and in WHO IS WHO IN Medicine and Healthcare. She is in private practice in San Bernardino California, and lives in Southern California.

For more information visit www.DrRuthTanyi.org, or to contact Dr Tanyi to speak at your event, church or non-Christian event, email her at: DrRuth@DrRuthTanyi.org, or call (909) 383 7978.

www.ingramcontent.com/pod-product-compliance
Lightning Source LLC
LaVergne TN
LVHW091310080426
835510LV00007B/443